W9-AAD-674

# CAREER QUIZZES

## 12 Tests to Help You Discover and Develop Your Dream Career

**John J. Liptak, Ed.D.**

jist Works
America's Career Publisher

**Career Quizzes: 12 Tests to Help You Discover and Develop Your Dream Career**

© 2008 by John J. Liptak

Published by JIST Works, an imprint of JIST Publishing
7321 Shadeland Station, Suite 200
Indianapolis, IN 46256-3923
Phone: 800-648-JIST          Fax: 877-454-7839
E-mail: info@jist.com          Web site: www.jist.com

Visit our Web site at **www.jist.com.** Find out about our products, get free tables of contents and sample pages, order a catalog, and link to other career-related sites.

Quantity discounts are available for JIST books. Please call 800-648-JIST or visit www.jist.com for a free catalog and more information.

Trade Product Manager: Lori Cates Hand
Development Editor: Dave Anderson
Copy Editor: Christopher Stolle
Project Editors: Lori Cates Hand and Aaron Black
Cover and Interior Designer: Toi Davis
Cover Illustration: Alwyn Cooper/iStockphoto
Proofreaders: Susan Shaw Dunn, Jeanne Clark
Indexer: Cheryl Lenser

Printed in the United States of America

13  12  11  10          9  8  7  6  5  4  3

Library of Congress Cataloging-in-Publication Data

Liptak, John J.
    Career quizzes : 12 tests to help you discover and develop your dream career / John J. Liptak.
        p. cm.
    Includes index.
    ISBN 978-1-59357-444-4 (alk. paper)
    1.  Vocational interests--Testing. 2.  Vocational guidance.  I. Title.
    HF5381.5.L568 2008
    153.9'4--dc22
                                2008010829

We have been careful to provide accurate information throughout this book, but it is possible that errors and omissions have been introduced. Please consider this in making any career plans or other important decisions. Trust your own judgment above all else and in all things.

ISBN 978-1-59357-444-4

# Acknowledgments

Writing this book has been an extraordinary and rewarding experience. First and foremost, my deepest gratitude goes to my career clients, who have granted me the privilege of working with them. I want to thank them for letting me be a part of their career journeys and for trusting me to share their stories, dreams, hardships, and successes. They have taught me most of what I know about the skills necessary to manage a career. I will be forever grateful.

I want to thank the following people for their generous contributions during the writing of this book. Most importantly, I would like to thank my editor at JIST Publishing, Dave Anderson, for his attention to detail, advice, and steadfast devotion to this project. I am grateful for his skillful editorial direction, friendship, and intuitive insights.

I would also like to thank Sue Pines, publisher at JIST Publishing, who understood the promise of this book from the beginning. Without her encouragement and support, this book would not have been possible. I am indebted to my agent, Jill Marsal of the Sandra Dijkstra Literary Agency, for believing in me, wisely advising me during this project, and for inspiring my very best work.

Finally, I would like to thank my wife, Kathy, who has supported me during the writing of this book. I love her very much, and I owe her a special debt of gratitude for her support, patience, and encouragement.

# About This Book

In my work as a career counselor, I have helped people resolve a wide variety of career-related problems. I have helped stay-at-home parents transition to new careers with little or no work experience, ex-offenders looking for their first job out of prison, and hundreds of people who had recently been "let go." The most difficult type of client, though, has to be the person who, as Henry David Thoreau puts it, "leads a life of quiet desperation." These are people who feel trapped in work that doesn't excite them, fit their interests, use their skills, or fulfill their needs—who while away the hours wondering if there isn't something better.

People like James, who at age 32 was experiencing a career crisis when he came into my office. James was a district manager with a well-respected fast-food franchise. He was rewarded with a respectable salary, good benefits, and a nice pension.

And he was miserable.

When I sat to talk with James, I began to understand his situation and the situation of all the other quiet, desperate souls like him. His work provided little opportunity for real leadership, initiative, or creativity. It had become tedious, repetitive, and mechanical. He wanted work that fit his personality and contributed to his self-esteem—work that was fulfilling and—dare he say it—enjoyable. And he's not the only one. Only about 10 percent of people report loving the work they do; the vast majority of people work at jobs where they experience limited career satisfaction or no satisfaction at all.

James needed to find his purpose, to develop a career that would be more gratifying, and to take action to make it happen. Most people put little or no time into planning and managing a career. Left to their own devices, most people find themselves in jobs that don't match their interests or talents or that don't fulfill their needs or bring them any closer to reaching their lifelong goals. They need guidance. They need a plan.

That was how the idea for this book was born. For the first time, the assessments that I use to take my clients through the career-coaching process are available to you in this book. A successful and rewarding career is possible, but you must take the time to do some self-reflection and self-exploration to get there.

If you have dreamed about work in which you are motivated, inspired, respected by colleagues, and paid well, you are not alone. By taking the 12 easy tests in this book, you take the first steps toward discovering and developing a fulfilling career and living the life you deserve.

# Table of Contents

# INTRODUCTION

# Achieving Career Satisfaction

If you're reading this, then the odds are you're looking for something—a new job or even a new career, a new path and a sense of direction, or a way to make a long-standing dream come true.

And you're certainly not alone. Studies have found that only about 50 percent of all workers are actually satisfied with their jobs. Job dissatisfaction is widespread among Americans of all educational levels, income brackets, and ethnic groups. People want more opportunities for career development, more ownership in decision making, greater work/life balance, and to be more highly valued as employees. Mostly, they just want rewarding work.

Career satisfaction is possible, but it requires you to know what truly motivates you. Many people will tell you that they're unhappy in their current job, but they can't pinpoint why. They talk about being unfulfilled, underutilized, or underpaid. Many will simply say they're "missing something." More often than not, a lack of job satisfaction is a matter of internal needs not being met—such as a lack of personal growth or a lack of opportunity to be creative—rather than external needs, such as pay or benefits. Thus, achieving job satisfaction is not simply a matter of earning a higher salary (although most of us wouldn't complain) but a matter of discovering the kind of work that matches your values and personality and fulfills all your needs.

Many different factors can influence your level of job satisfaction, including pay and benefits, the opportunity to use your skills and abilities, the level of challenge you feel in doing your job, the quality of leadership, the quality of your social relationships, and the variety of duties you perform. Knowing which of these is most important to you can give you insight into which direction to take your career.

# How Satisfied Are You?

Before we get too far, let's see how satisfied you are. The following assessment, or "quiz," consists of 25 items describing personal feelings and reactions you might have toward your current job or toward past jobs. Respond to each item using the following scale:

| Always True | Somewhat True | Seldom True | Never True |
|:-:|:-:|:-:|:-:|
| **0** | **1** | **2** | **3** |

1. I am often bored at work    0    1    (2)    3

In the above example, the circled 2 indicates that the statement is **Seldom True** for the person completing the assessment. If you are currently unemployed, think back to your last job as you respond to the following items. This is not a test, and there are no right or wrong answers. Be sure to respond to every statement.

| | Always True | Somewhat True | Seldom True | Never True |
|---|:-:|:-:|:-:|:-:|
| 1. I am often bored at work | 0 | 1 | (2) | 3 |
| 2. I watch the clock while working | (0) | 1 | 2 | 3 |
| 3. I see no value in the work I do | 0 | 1 | (2) | 3 |
| 4. I never look forward to going to work | 0 | (1) | 2 | 3 |
| 5. I often think of ways to get out of work | 0 | (1) | 2 | 3 |
| 6. I do not use all my abilities at work | 0 | (1) | 2 | 3 |
| 7. I do not want to learn more about my job | 0 | 1 | (2) | 3 |
| 8. I have already mentally quit my job | 0 | (1) | 2 | 3 |
| 9. I go home immediately when the workday is over | 0 | (1) | 2 | 3 |
| 10. I am not ambitious at work | 0 | (1) | 2 | 3 |
| 11. I feel exhausted at the end of the workday | (0) | 1 | 2 | 3 |
| 12. I spend a lot of time at work making personal calls | 0 | 1 | 2 | (3) |
| 13. I use my vacation time very quickly | 0 | (1) | 2 | 3 |
| 14. I feel unappreciated at work | 0 | (1) | 2 | 3 |
| 15. I would never recommend the work I do to others | 0 | 1 | (2) | 3 |
| 16. If I hit the lottery, I would immediately quit my job | (0) | 1 | 2 | 3 |
| 17. I often miss work due to illness | 0 | 1 | 2 | (3) |
| 18. I often feel stressed at work | 0 | (1) | 2 | 3 |
| 19. I often worry about my work when I am not there | 0 | 1 | 2 | (3) |
| 20. I often daydream of having a different job | 0 | (1) | 2 | 3 |

| | Always True | Somewhat True | Seldom True | Never True |
|---|:---:|:---:|:---:|:---:|
| 21. I find myself doing things that I hope will get me fired | 0 | 1 | 2 | (3) |
| 22. I spend a lot of time at work surfing the Internet | 0 | 1 | 2 | (3) |
| 23. I feel like I am underpaid | (0) | 1 | 2 | 3 |
| 24. My work is not that challenging | 0 | 1 | (2) | 3 |
| 25. There is no room for personal growth at work | 0 | 1 | (2) | 3 |

Total: ___37___

Now add the scores you circled and put that total on the line marked Total at the end of the assessment.

Scores from 0–25 indicate a **low** degree of job satisfaction. If you scored in the low range, then you should take some measures to improve your satisfaction at work or find a job that better meets your needs. In fact, a complete career change might be in order. Thankfully, the rest of this book can coach you through the process of finding and developing a satisfying career.

Scores from 26–50 indicate that you are experiencing an **average** degree of job satisfaction. We all have things we like and dislike about our jobs, and these tend to balance out and make work bearable. But such a job will seldom reap the bigger internal rewards that lead to career fulfillment. At the very least, you should try to find ways to enhance your satisfaction at your current job or in your current line of work, but a career change isn't out of the question either. Use this book to help you make long-term career plans that will lead to more rewards.

Scores from 51–75 indicate a **high** degree of job satisfaction. But even a perfect score on this assessment doesn't mean there isn't room for improvement. The remainder of this book can help you enhance your job satisfaction even more!

# The Quest for Satisfaction

Work satisfaction is the never-ending quest for self-fulfillment and self-actualization. And it began thousands of years ago with a man named Socrates. Socrates was an extraordinary Greek philosopher who made it his mission to help other people develop a deeper understanding of what constituted a good life. He dedicated himself to discovering wisdom within himself and drawing this wisdom out of others. His approach, called the Socratic method, consisted of a series of questions he would pose to help other people explore their true nature so they could experience success.

I'm no Socrates, but in my career-counseling practice, I have found that successful people are able to grow personally and professionally by devoting themselves to lifelong learning, self-exploration, reflection, and growth. Successful people constantly invent and reinvent themselves based on a process of constant self-assessment.

Successful people have a rare ability to celebrate their strengths and face up to their weaknesses. They make effective decisions based on self-knowledge and take action to make changes in their lives. Research suggests that those people who significantly invest in themselves and their own growth and development generally experience greater levels of career and life fulfillment than those who merely wait for opportunities to come along.

The qualities needed to become successful are within each and every one of us, regardless of race, age, class, or educational level. This book, and the assessments and exercises it contains, adheres to Socrates' mantra that "the unexamined life is not worth living." It will help you examine and explore the enduring qualities or characteristics you possess and how those characteristics affect your career development.

# The Guided Self-Reflection Approach

*Career Quizzes* is unlike most other career success books, largely because it does not pretend to provide you with a magic formula for success. In reality, you have to work for it, hence the tests mentioned in the title.

But they aren't really tests (not in the panic-inducing, late-night-cramming sense of the word). They are self-assessments that can help you explore your goals and values, skills and abilities, and plans and purposes. Assessments can help you recognize patterns of behavior, identify strategies that are productive and unproductive, and enrich your understanding of how you interact with the world. Assessments provide a path to self-discovery through the exploration of what makes you unique. I call this *guided self-reflection.*

Guided self-reflection is a unique way of learning about yourself. Each chapter of this book will coach you through the self-reflection process. In each chapter, you will:

- Identify barriers to your career success.

- Complete assessments to learn more about yourself.

- Explore your results and find meaning in them.

- Devise new strategies and plans based on what you've learned.

- Commit to making the changes required to achieve more career success.

Be aware that the assessments in this book are exercises in self-exploration and not final definitions of your character or attitudes. Still, the results of this process should help you reflect on your life, question past behaviors, find meaning, and make connections. You will then be encouraged to set goals and take action.

# The Four Steps to Success

*Career Quizzes* guides you through the career-coaching process as it relates to four critical areas of career management:

1. **Find Your Purpose.** Most people spend a lifetime trying to find their calling in life. The assessments included in Part I of this book can help you do just that by guiding you to define the needs you want your career to meet and helping you discover the path that will best lead to fulfilling your purpose.

2. **Identify Your Ideal Job.** Since you were a child, people have probably been asking you what you want to be when you grow up. You might still be trying to answer this question. Identifying your purpose is one thing, but finding the ideal job to help you achieve your purpose can seem even more difficult. According to the U.S. Department of Labor, there are approximately 20,000 different jobs available in the workplace. To find the best one, you must take a serious look at yourself and how your characteristics match with the opportunities available. The assessments in Part II will help you narrow that list of jobs from 20,000 to a mere handful (or at least two handfuls) by taking a close look at your interests, values, skills, and personality.

3. **Develop a Career Plan.** Even people who have an idea of what they want to do with their lives lack a career plan and well-defined career goals to get them there. Part III will help you make effective career decisions—choosing among the many alternatives you may be considering—and then help you develop a plan to achieve your career goals. You will also learn how to achieve the proper balance between your life and your career as you pursue those goals.

4. **Take Action.** A plan is useful only if you follow it. The assessments in part IV will help you develop an effective job search campaign and take action. You will learn more about your personality style in searching for a job, what your job search strengths and weaknesses are, and ways you can improve them to reach your goals more effectively. Finally, you will discover what you can do to ensure your ongoing career success.

# A Word About the Assessments in This Book

An assessment can provide you with valuable information about yourself, but please remember that such instruments cannot measure everything about you. The purpose of these assessments is not to pigeonhole you, but to help you explore your personal preferences and characteristics and how they impact your career development. Remember that this book also contains *assessments* and not tests, at least not in the traditional sense. Traditional tests measure whether something is right or wrong. For the exercises in this book, there are no right or wrong answers. The questions require only your opinions or attitudes about a topic of importance in your career and your life.

Keep in mind that the assessments in this book are based on self-reported data. In other words, the accuracy and usefulness of the information depends on the information that you provide about yourself. You may not learn much from taking some of these assessments, or you might simply verify information that you already knew. On the other hand, you may uncover the key to your dissatisfaction or the pathway to your future success.

Moreover, the assessments in this book are merely a starting point for you to learn more about yourself and how you fit into the world. You may not always agree with the outcomes, so remember that these are exploratory exercises and not a final definition of who you are or what you believe. Lastly, the exercises in this book are not a substitute for professional assistance. If you feel you need additional help, please consult a professional career counselor.

As you complete the assessments in this book, remember to do the following:

- Take your time completing the tests. There is no time limit, so work at your own pace. Allow yourself time to reflect on your results and how they compare to what you already know about yourself.

- Find a quiet place where you can complete the tests without being disturbed.

- Do not answer the assessment questions as you think others would like you to answer them or how you think others see you. Remember that these assessments help you reflect on your life and explore some of the barriers that keep you from attaining career success.

- Assessments are powerful tools—as long as you are honest with yourself. Be truthful in your responses so that your results are an honest reflection of you.

- Complete the exercises included after each assessment. These exercises will allow you to explore how the results of each assessment can be integrated into your personal and career development.

- Finally, remember that self-discovery and career planning can be fun. Don't stress over the assessments or the results. Just learn as much about yourself as you can. You will enjoy taking the assessments, and you will learn a lot about yourself and your goals in the process.

We all have our own definition of success, whether it's having a lucrative career, becoming renowned for our work, owning our own business, or helping other people. This book will help you explore what success means to you and make plans to achieve that success. By taking five minutes out of your day to complete just one assessment in this book, you take one more step toward realizing your dreams.

# PART I: DEFINE YOUR PURPOSE

*"The future belongs to those who believe in the beauty of their dreams!"*
—Eleanor Roosevelt

# CHAPTER 1

# Making a Change

*"If you don't know where you're going, you'll end up somewhere else."*
*—Yogi Berra*

Your career is much more than the work you do, but the work you do plays an integral part. You spend more time at work than engaging in any other activity. If you work 40 hours a week for 40 years, you will spend a total of 83,200 hours at your job. Of course, in today's workplace, many people spend 50 or more hours per week at work–more than 100,000 hours in their lifetimes. And many people do not consider those 100,000 hours "time well spent." If you are not happy in your work, you will not experience much career or life satisfaction. Your career is your purpose in life–the lasting imprint that you leave on the world. It should be worth your time.

If you are reading this book, odds are it is time for a shift in your career. Change and transition can take many forms. It can be unexpected or planned, initiated from within or imposed from without, accepted with open arms or fought against with tooth and claw. This chapter will examine both the internal and external factors that prompt people to make a career change.

But first, consider some current statistics offered by Mikela and Philip Tarlow in their ground-breaking book *Digital Aboriginal:*

- More than 50 percent of all workers report dissatisfaction with their current jobs.

- Twenty-five percent of all workers are actively considering changing their careers.

- More than 50 percent of all workers would consider a drop in pay if their jobs became more meaningful.

- Seventy-five percent of all workers would take a pay cut in order to have more personal time.

- Fifty percent of all workers are experiencing symptoms of burnout.

- Between 15 and 25 percent of all workers have voluntarily accepted a cut in pay to downscale, simplify, and engage in a less materialistic lifestyle. To some degree, they have simply dropped out of the rat race.

- When asked what would make them happy, 66 percent of all workers said they would spend more time with their families, whereas 47 percent said they felt they would be happier if they could make a difference in their communities.

Workers today have reached a point where they want meaning more than anything else in their careers. They crave purpose, a sense of direction, and a feeling that they make the world a better place. And if you are one of them, then it is probably time for a change.

This chapter will help you identify how you respond to the ever-changing workplace, how you cope with change, and the steps you can take to confront your career transition with the right attitude. After all, if you don't go into your transition with the right outlook, you might end up back where you started.

# A World of Change

Our lives consist of a never-ending series of transitions. We can expect and prepare for such transitions, but that doesn't necessarily make them easy. Even if a transition is welcome, it can still cause anxiety and concern. When transitions are not welcome–like losing your job–the emotions and demands placed on you are even more intense. To overcome this anxiety, you need to develop transition skills so that you can respond quickly and flexibly to new career demands.

Economists and scholars suggest that we are in the middle of a workplace revolution. The dynamics of this new workplace have affected most workers at one time or another, and they are probably affecting you. External forces–from a corporate restructuring to an economic downturn to the rise of globalization–play a part in accelerating change in your personal and work lives. Whether it's a move to a new office or a move to a new state or taking a year off to write a book or five years to raise children, change is never a question of if. It is more often a question of, "What now?"

Much of our changing landscape stems from new technology, which continually creates new opportunities and new problems in the workforce. Entire industries continue to emerge and explode as a result of technological advances–from video games to biotechnology. Thanks to the Internet, more workers are skipping the morning commute and instead working from home. Like most revolutions, the technological one comes at a cost, expressed most directly in the loss of jobs. For example, my mother worked for Ma Bell as a telephone operator many years ago, but she lost her job to an automated telephone-answering service. And so it goes.

Organizations have also started to change the way they employ workers. Wages over the last decade have steadily declined for the average worker, and this trend will probably continue. In addition, employers often pay less toward employee pension plans and health insurance costs, which means employees shoulder more of the burden. To cut costs and improve efficiency, most major companies have increased their use of temporary workers, like consultants or freelancers, or outsource them to countries with lower labor costs. Experts suggest that at least a third of all job roles are in transition, a third of all vocational-technical schools have become obsolete, and a third of all workers eventually leave their jobs.

Fifty years ago, people worked for the same employer their entire career, and the average tenure for a person in a job was 23 years. By 1996, that figure had dropped to about 4 years. If you are just now entering the workforce, you have at least 12 different jobs to look forward to–and probably more. In the future, many workers will change jobs more frequently, will move more often to find a job, and will require additional training as a way of moving into new employment opportunities. In the past, "job hoppers" were not considered loyal or trustworthy.

> **NOTE**
>
> If you are considering a change (or if one has been forced on you), you need to prepare for the transition. Learning to deal effectively with career transitions is the first step on your path to career success.

Nowadays, those same people are "savvy career managers," building their skill sets as they search for their true calling.

## Making Career Transitions

Career change is inevitable but embraceable–provided you have a sense of direction and the right attitude. All people experience career transitions. Depending on the circumstances, career transitions may be voluntary or involuntary, desired or undesired. But the results of such changes–where you end up transitioning to–are ultimately up to you.

Not too long ago, I found myself in the middle of a major career transition–one of several. I had been working in a state prison in Delaware, helping offenders prepare for transitions of their own as part of a reentry counseling program. I had also been working as an instructor at a local college in the evenings. When a full-time teaching position became available, I applied and received a job offer.

> **NOTE**
>
> Always be prepared for career transitions. The more aware you are of yourself and how you fit into the world of work, the less surprised you will be when a career transition is thrust on you.

That was the easy part. Making the transition from the prison setting to a college setting was the hard part. I was used to working in a very structured environment (most teachers don't have the benefit of armed guards watching over their students). After my first few days as a college professor, one of my colleagues took pity on me and told me that I didn't have to sit in the office all day when I wasn't teaching–after my office hours, I could go home. That represented just one of hundreds of smaller changes that came with that transition. Teaching in a prison and teaching in a college classroom are vastly different affairs (although some of my college students would disagree)–each with its own unique challenges. Recognizing those challenges, accepting them, and finding ways to overcome them were the keys to making a successful transition.

Career transitions rarely happen smoothly. Even changes that you want–like that much-desired promotion–may mean that you will have to develop new relationships, leave behind old ones, work more hours, take fewer vacations, or learn new skills. Navigating such a transition requires careful planning and decision making, but it also calls for an increased self-awareness. Knowing how you are likely to react to those changes can help you better prepare for them.

---

### THE FOUR STAGES OF A TRANSITION

Most people pass through four distinct stages during a career transition. The speed and urgency of your path through these stages will differ from those of other people, and you may move so quickly through a stage that it seems like you were never in it.

**Stage I: Denial.** Regardless of whether a transition is positive or negative, a general refusal to accept the reality of it helps us protect ourselves from being overwhelmed. Take Mike, an accountant facing imminent downsizing as word spreads that the corporation he works for might decide to move its operations to India. In this phase, Mike insists that it is only a rumor and that he will wait it out and things will blow over, while his colleagues begin polishing their resumes. The longer he stays in denial, the more he hinders his career.

**Stage II: Resistance.** In this stage, personal distress levels rise and we look for someone or something to blame. We focus on the past rather than the future. Past denial but unemployed, Mike begins to blame everyone for his situation: He blames the people of India for being willing to work for less money than he does, he blames the corporation for being cheap and not caring about employees who have been faithful, and he blames his supervisors for not fighting for his job. He feels depressed about losing his job and can't find the motivation to look for a new one. Such feelings can build up and have dramatic effects on our physical and psychological well-being, from headaches to stress to insomnia. Successfully moving on from this stage, then, becomes an exercise in self-preservation.

**Stage III: Exploration.** In this phase, we begin to break free of the negativity and despair and shift into a more positive, future-oriented frame of mind. We come to the realization that we will survive the career transition and may even be stronger for it. Mike realizes that although he liked his job, he might like other jobs even better. He feels energized and starts to act on this newfound motivation. He begins to clarify his goals, assess his strengths and weaknesses, and explore alternatives and new possibilities.

**Stage IV: Commitment.** In this phase, we begin to focus on a new course of action. Mike begins to think about ways he could pursue a lifelong dream of entrepreneurship. He talks with people at the Small Business Administration about how he could start his own consulting business. When Mike's small-business loan finally comes through, he can't believe it–and a new transition cycle begins.

---

**NOTE**

Even if you think you know what direction you're going, this assessment can still be a valuable tool for verifying that direction. The more you know about yourself, the easier it is to make the right career decisions.

# The Career Transition Scale

People experiencing career transitions are often confused about how to navigate them. The following assessment can help people who know they need to do something but aren't exactly sure what. It can help you determine, based on your personality, which career direction might be best for you to pursue.

Read each statement and decide how true the statement is for you. This is not a test. Since there are no right or wrong answers, do not spend too much time on each item. Be sure to respond honestly to every statement.

| | Very True | Somewhat True | Not True |
|---|---|---|---|
| 1. I would like to stay in one profession my entire career | 3 | 2 | (1) |
| 2. I am interested in part-time work | 3 | (2) | 1 |
| 3. I am always alert to business opportunities | 3 | 2 | (1) |
| 4. I get bored and lose interest easily | 3 | (2) | 1 |
| 5. I do not like change | 3 | 2 | (1) |
| 6. I would willingly take less pay to work fewer hours | (3) | 2 | 1 |
| 7. I often have two or more sources of income | 3 | 2 | (1) |
| 8. I quickly adapt to new situations | (3) | 2 | 1 |
| 9. I would describe myself as very practical | 3 | (2) | 1 |
| 10. I gain satisfaction from both work and leisure activities | 3 | 2 | (1) |
| 11. I am a risk-taker | 3 | 2 | (1) |
| 12. I do not mind changing jobs | 3 | (2) | 1 |
| 13. I easily commit to my employer's product or service | 3 | (2) | 1 |
| 14. I have many different hobbies | 3 | 2 | (1) |
| 15. I always attempt to find ways to meet an employer's needs | 3 | (2) | 1 |
| 16. I like to gain experience by working at different jobs | 3 | (2) | 1 |
| 17. I would like to stay with the same employer my entire career | 3 | 2 | (1) |
| 18. I work so I can pursue my hobbies | 3 | 2 | (1) |
| 19. I am very goal oriented | 3 | 2 | (1) |
| 20. I constantly network for new job opportunities | 3 | 2 | (1) |
| 21. My work is my primary source of life satisfaction | 3 | 2 | (1) |
| 22. I seek recognition and success from both work and leisure | 3 | 2 | (1) |
| 23. I have always wanted to own my own company | 3 | 2 | (1) |
| 24. When a job loses its challenge, I move on to another | 3 | 2 | (1) |
| 25. I prefer a highly structured work environment | 3 | (2) | 1 |
| 26. Work is not a problem–as long as it does not interfere with the rest of my life | 3 | (2) | 1 |
| 27. I have skills that I can transfer from one job to another | 3 | (2) | 1 |
| 28. I believe that self-promotion is critical to career development | 3 | (2) | 1 |
| 29. I feel a sense of connection to my work | 3 | (2) | 1 |
| 30. I carefully balance my work and personal life | 3 | 2 | (1) |

*(continued)*

*(continued)*

|  | Very True | Somewhat True | Not True |
|---|---|---|---|
| 31. Others consider me to be a visionary thinker | 3 | 2 | (1) |
| 32. Changing jobs is a way to build new skill sets | 3 | (2) | 1 |
| 33. I will stick with an employer through good and bad times | 3 | (2) | 1 |
| 34. I am an idea person | 3 | (2) | 1 |
| 35. I am highly competitive | 3 | 2 | (1) |
| 36. I need to keep finding new challenges | 3 | (2) | 1 |
| 37. I always worry about losing my job | 3 | 2 | (1) |
| 38. I have lots of interests competing for my time | 3 | 2 | (1) |
| 39. I would like to build a business from scratch | 3 | 2 | (1) |
| 40. I cannot imagine staying with the same company for decades | (3) | 2 | 1 |

## Scoring

The Career Transition Scale is designed to measure how you deal with career transitions–otherwise known as your *career transition style.*

Use the spaces below to record the number that you circled for each item in the assessment. Calculate the totals for each column (scale) and then put that total underneath each column.

| Scale I | Scale II | Scale III | Scale IV |
|---|---|---|---|
| 1 _____ | 2 _____ | 3 _____ | 4 _____ |
| 5 _____ | 6 _____ | 7 _____ | 8 _____ |
| 9 _____ | 10 _____ | 11 _____ | 12 _____ |
| 13 _____ | 14 _____ | 15 _____ | 16 _____ |
| 17 _____ | 18 _____ | 19 _____ | 20 _____ |
| 21 _____ | 22 _____ | 23 _____ | 24 _____ |
| 25 _____ | 26 _____ | 27 _____ | 28 _____ |
| 29 _____ | 30 _____ | 31 _____ | 32 _____ |
| 33 _____ | 34 _____ | 35 _____ | 36 _____ |
| 37 _____ | 38 _____ | 39 _____ | 40 _____ |
| **Total Traditionalist** | **Total Catalyst** | **Total Opportunist** | **Total Job Jumper** |
| _____ | _____ | _____ | _____ |

Each section corresponds to one possible approach to career development and, thus, one way to navigate your current transition. A low score on any scale (10—16) suggests that this is probably not the best direction for you. On the flip side, a high score on a scale (24—30) suggests that this is an approach that you should seriously consider, as it best matches your personality and your current philosophy regarding your career.

# Making Your Career Transition

A greater awareness of how your personality fits your career development style can provide you with a much-needed sense of direction. The following profiles provide information related to each way of dealing with career transitions. Start with the scale in which you scored the highest. If you scored high on more than one scale, you may have more than one way to deal effectively with a career transition. Read each description and then explore the suggestions that follow; they will help you set goals to better manage your career.

Some of the following types may seem to have an easier time with career transitions than others. The real key, however, is to make a transition that fits with your own needs, goals, values, and interests. That's the goal of this chapter and, in fact, the entire book.

## *The Traditionalist: Working for the Gold Watch*

Traditionalists are interested in sticking with one occupation–sometimes even one employer–for their entire career. They tend to be very conventional (some might even say "old fashioned") in their approach to employment and career development. They view loyalty to an organization as highly important. Although their relationship with the company may not be perfect, it provides them with a sense of continuity, comfort, and security. Thus, any threat of separation from the company can seem stressful.

A traditionalist's job is her primary source of satisfaction and identity, and she will do almost anything to preserve it. She can make changes when learning to work with new supervisors and coworkers and can make great interpersonal adjustments in times of transition by being diplomatic. Traditionalists are most interested in growing with a job, moving up the ladder, and achieving the highest level of success within their chosen field.

---

### SUSIE TRADITIONALIST

When Susie was let go from her sales job because of a corporate merger, she was shaken up. Most everyone else in the company had moved on and started to look for new jobs, but she was determined not to leave without a fight. She put together a portfolio of her work to show the new company owners. She made an appointment and gave them her best sales pitch. She provided sample products she had developed, spouted sales statistics to support her case, and showed thank-you letters from satisfied customers. Not surprisingly, the new owners decided to retain her in her old position with the new company, with the potential to move up even higher in the organization.

## The Advantages of Being a Traditionalist

- Traditionalists typically believe that work can meet most or all of their needs.

- Traditionalists feel a strong sense of connection to their work and to their employers.

- Traditionalists are highly motivated and enthusiastic about the work they do. They tend to have a great work ethic.

- Traditionalists possess well-honed political skills that allow them to function effectively with new administrators and coworkers.

- Traditionalists understand the value of moving up in an organization and look for ways to make an impact and get noticed.

## The Disadvantages of Being a Traditionalist

- Traditionalists often pass up great opportunities in other companies because of their loyalty to their current employer.

- Traditionalists often live in a state of denial when faced with a forced career transition.

- Traditionalists meet almost all their needs at work. Thus, work becomes their primary passion–often to the neglect of other life roles.

- When faced with job loss, traditionalists may have a harder time recovering and finding new job opportunities.

## Strategies for Career Development

Traditionalists facing a career transition need to carefully consider their current interests, needs, and values. After all, if your goal is to find one occupation and even one organization that you hope to stick with until retirement, it is important that you like what you do, that it meets all your needs, that it provides opportunity for growth, and that it will continue to challenge you. If you are in the middle of a job loss or face that possibility, don't be afraid to fight for your job–tenacity can pay off. If you desire a career change, find a company that is growing or has a record of stability. You should search for organizations with lots of opportunity for advancement. Take your time in deciding which company to work for.

Once there, the key to maintaining a traditionalist career path is to convince your employer that you want to move up. Make yourself integral to the company's success. The following suggestions can help you identify ways that you can be more valuable to an organization:

- Identify problems that you can solve. Look around your organization to see where it could operate more effectively or efficiently.

- Invent a brand-new service or product. By being innovative, you will have a better chance of advancing.

- Learn more effective emotional intelligence skills, such as conflict resolution, communication, time management, and leadership skills.

- Identify your competitive advantage. What do you do better than anyone else?

- Set goals for yourself. Periodically reassess where you are in your job and what you can do improve the quality of your work and get noticed.

---

**EXERCISE**

In the space below, write down some specific things you can do to ensure a traditionalist career path (if you are so inclined):

_____

_____

_____

_____

---

# The Catalyst: Going to Work in Order to Play

In chemistry, catalysts speed along chemical reactions; they are a means to an end. In career development terms, catalysts are those who use their work as a means to engage in other pleasures and fulfill other life goals. They seek out multiple paths to overall life satisfaction; they commit to many different work and leisure activities–all of which have the potential to make them happy. If one activity disappears, the catalyst turns to the next one for satisfaction. For this reason, catalysts do not fear career transitions.

Although they appreciate the financial security that comes with steady employment, unlike the traditionalist, they are not "married" to a job. They tend to maintain a job so that they can discover and engage in new and exciting leisure activities. They prefer to work less than most people and would gladly trade more time off for less money. Because they have so many diverse interests, work is not always–or often–their first priority.

---

**JACK CATALYST**

Jack is a bank manager who writes travel articles as a hobby. His job as a manager provides him with the money to own a home, buy nice clothes, and eat out at nice restaurants. It offers him safety and security for his future. However, being a bank manager doesn't come close to satisfying all his interests or life goals. Therefore, he turns to his other interests–traveling and writing. On the weekends, Jack enjoys taking short trips up and down the East Coast. He writes about his travels and has even sold some of his stories to *Coastal Living* magazine. On his vacations, he enjoys taking trips to Europe and learning as much as he can about other cultures. He takes Spanish language classes at a local community college and plans to also learn German, Italian, and Japanese. Someday he hopes to write a book documenting his travels in foreign countries.

## The Advantages of Being a Catalyst

- Catalysts recognize the importance of integrating their interests with their careers. Their leisure activities are a vital part of their career plan and provide a constant source of satisfaction.

- Catalysts tend to focus more on personal growth and development. They view success in terms of accumulating experiences.

- Catalysts enjoy their work and are committed to it, but it takes much more than work for them to feel fulfilled.

## The Disadvantages of Being a Catalyst

- Catalysts sometimes take on too many interests. Thus, they often cannot engage in any of them with the depth they would like.

- Catalysts often become so attached to their leisure activities that they let their work suffer. For the catalyst, a work-leisure balance is critical. They often become complacent in a job and overlook opportunities for more challenging work. Thus, they are less likely to move up within an organization.

- Catalysts may be too eager for career transitions in their lives. They see these transitions as a way of starting over–to redevelop their career plan and pursue new opportunities. The problem is that this often leads to instability; for example, moving frequently or uprooting children from friends and schools.

## Strategies for Career Development

Catalysts facing a career transition need to develop a lifestyle plan that integrates all their various work, leisure, and educational interests. For catalysts, an ideal job will probably be one that allows them to maintain their interests in a wide variety of leisure activities while providing some meaning and purpose at work. Catalysts should be patient in searching for the ideal job that provides them with this type of balance between work and leisure time.

Balancing work and leisure isn't easy (as chapter 9 will tell you); however, it is crucial for people who see their work as a means to explore their leisure interests. The key to maintaining a catalyst career path is to find ways to integrate your leisure interests into your work or to find ways to better manage the time you spend on each. The following suggestions can help:

- Identify at least five occupations and leisure activities that match your personality.

- Think about ways you can reduce the time you spend working so that you will have more time for leisure activities. For example, could you ask for more time off for less money, or find seasonal or part-time work?

- Try to turn a hobby into an employment opportunity. For example, if you enjoy playing with dogs in your spare time, could you start a dog-sitting business on the weekends?

- Take a sheet of paper and make two columns labeled "Work" and "Leisure." Identify all the potential work activities you might enjoy and all the potential leisure activities you might enjoy. Then explore ways that you could turn work into leisure and leisure into work.

---

**EXERCISE**

In the space below, write down some specific things you can do to ensure a catalyst career path (if you are so inclined):

_____

_____

_____

_____

---

# The Opportunist: Ready for Whatever Comes Along

Opportunists take an entrepreneurial approach to their work. They are risk-takers and innovators. They are goal oriented and always on alert for new and exciting business opportunities. Opportunists concentrate on constantly improving their skills and finding ways to apply those skills to new ventures. They are willing to start over–spending the time and effort to build a business from scratch, for example–if the rewards seem worth it. They are highly competitive and work hard to succeed in the enterprise *du jour.*

Opportunists view career transitions as opportunities to make more money, be promoted to a better position, gain more prestige, or start a business of their own. They have an intuitive sense for when things are about to change and often have "backup" plans. Because of that, they tend to accept change with greater ease than others, viewing them as occasions for growth.

---

**KARMA OPPORTUNIST**

Karma's artistic abilities have taken her down many different career paths. She studied art education in college, and her interest in ceramics and stained glass took her to England, where she worked with some of the best in the field. She eventually came back to the United States, where she took a job teaching art at a high school. After six years of teaching, she had saved enough money to open her own studio. Now she sells her pottery and stained glass in her studio and through arts-and-crafts shows. Her years of teaching gave her the experience she needed to offer art lessons to children and adults three days a week. Eventually, she hopes to teach her craft at the local community college while also expanding her studio into an online business. That is, unless something even better comes along.

## The Advantages of Being an Opportunist

- Opportunists have a true gift for identifying career prospects, whether inside their organization, in competing companies, or in their own business startups.

- Opportunists find challenge in doing new and different things.

- Opportunists can see the connections between things. They have an intuitive sense of when and how opportunities in the workplace can lead to business ventures for them personally.

- Opportunists are not afraid to take risks. However, they are usually smart enough to have contingency plans.

## The Disadvantages of Being an Opportunist

- Opportunists live in the future. They spend so much time looking for the next new opportunity that they may have a hard time being effective in their current job.

- Opportunists can take too many risks. They like to calculate the likelihood of success in a career transition or business endeavor; however, that can be difficult to gauge in today's ever-changing workplace.

- Opportunists have a harder time being content. They are always so busy thinking about the next opportunity that they lose sight of current rewards.

## Strategies for Career Development

Opportunists facing a possible career transition need to be open to innovation. They can use a career transition as an opportunity to improve their skills, move ahead in an industry, or start their own business enterprise. It can be helpful for opportunists to think of a career transition as a personal challenge and find ways to overcome it.

Being an opportunist in a land of opportunity is one thing, but not everyone has a new career venture knocking on his or her door. The key to maintaining an opportunist career path is to make your own opportunities rather than simply wait for one to come along. The following suggestions can help:

- Consider self-employment opportunities. Determine what type of business you would like to start and research what it would take to get started (be sure to read chapter 3).

- Consider doing freelance or consulting work to supplement your income and gain more experience.

- Continuously research other career opportunities that might offer more rewards.

- Network with people in your industry so that you can rise up the ranks faster.

- Focus on improving your transferable skills. When the right opportunity does come along, you want to ensure you are qualified for it.

---

### EXERCISE

In the space below, write down some specific things you can do to ensure an opportunist career path (if you are so inclined):

_____

_____

_____

_____

---

# The Job Jumper: Finding Satisfaction, One Job at a Time

Job jumpers get bored doing the same work and seek out new occupations where they can learn and use new skills. Change is a way of life for them; they rarely see it as a *setback*–it's usually just more of a *shift*. Like opportunists, job jumpers are always networking and promoting themselves, but unlike opportunists, jumpers aren't looking for the *next best thing* as much as they are simply looking for something *different*.

Because of the transient nature of their careers, job jumpers don't worry about safety and security. They aren't even really concerned about being downsized and may be the most comfortable career development style in today's insecure working world. They thrive on change and want to transform the companies they work for much faster than traditionalist employees. Because they will work for several different companies in one industry, they tend to gain a broader perspective. Their range of experiences often qualifies them for a wide variety of jobs, but resumes full of different positions may be a turnoff for employers looking for a stable employee.

### STEVEN JOB JUMPER

Steven is a jumper. He went to college and earned a bachelor's degree in business and then started working in an employment agency. He worked at this job for three years and learned the business. Eventually, he heard about a job as a career counselor in a small college in his hometown, working with college students who are about to graduate. He convinced the hiring committee that his experience in the employment agency would benefit their students. As part of this new job, he could make contact with hundreds of human resource representatives interested in hiring that college's students. Whenever these representatives were on campus, Steven would go out of his way to meet and greet them, building his network of contacts. It wasn't long before he scored an interview for a better-paying coaching job with a private outplacement firm. It's a cushy job with great benefits, but even if he gets it, he doesn't intend to stay there for the rest of his life. He'll learn the business and develop new skills that he can market to another company, building his career piece by piece.

## The Advantages of Being a Job Jumper

- Job jumpers have a great deal of knowledge and experience that they have gained from working in other companies. They can often use this knowledge in product development and in strategic planning for a new company.

- Job jumpers have access to many contacts. Those who are good at networking are always aware of new employment opportunities.

- Job jumpers believe in having fun at work, and they invest considerable time in the people they meet; after all, the people they meet are possible sources of employment down the road.

- Job jumpers don't let themselves become bored. They don't stagnate in jobs that aren't good for them. Once they recognize that a job is not the right fit, they go find one that is.

## The Disadvantages of Being a Job Jumper

- Job jumpers are unreliable and are often viewed as such by employers (you can usually tell a jumper by an eclectic resume).

- Job jumpers are so interested in meeting people and networking that they forget to do the job at hand.

- Job jumpers show limited loyalty. They don't expect to be around forever and don't trust employers to look out for their best interests. They take what they can from a job and use it to find the next one.

## Strategies for Career Development

Job jumpers facing a possible career transition need to use it as an opportunity to learn new skills. Because they are accustomed to being in this type of situation, job jumpers will probably welcome the transition. They usually feel a sense of relief and excitement about finding a new place to work. They do not worry about the lack of security associated with a career transition.

At first glance, one might think job jumping is not a career development style but instead is a total lack of career management. Fifty years ago, that might have been the case, but today, job jumping has become *the way* to spend your 20s and 30s. Statistics show that the average person will hold 10 different jobs between the ages of 18 and 38. Job jumping represents a lack of planning only if you aren't doing it right–that is, if you aren't making careful career decisions based on what's right for you. The key to maintaining a successful job jumper career path is to build on your experiences and see how they all work together to make you more marketable. The following suggestions can help:

- Build your network. Start developing a list of all the prospective employers for whom you might like to work. Identify a hiring official in each business and then develop a plan for how you can meet that person.

- Create a portfolio of your achievements that you can show prospective employers.

- At every job you work, learn as many new skills as you can.

- Improve your interviewing skills. Convincing an employer to hire you might take some additional effort, especially given your unstable work history.

- Create your own Web site to market yourself. Headhunters are increasingly using electronic media to identify potential talent.

---

**EXERCISE**

In the space below, write down some specific things you can do to ensure a job jumper career path (if you are so inclined):

_____

_____

_____

_____

---

# Which Style Is Best?

Odds are, everyone will have an answer to this question based on his or her own preferences (or scores). Answers may vary by generation (baby boomers are more likely to appreciate a traditionalist approach), by interests (fun-loving, artistic types might trumpet the catalyst approach), and certainly based on one's past work history or current circumstance (it's hard to take a traditionalist stance when you've been downsized three times or a job jumper stance when you have children who need reliable health care). But the truth is that today's economy makes room for all types, and no single approach to career development is better than another. More likely than not, you will find and take more than one path through your career, adopting more than one approach as you go.

> **NOTE**
>
> Look at a career transition as the best thing that could happen to you. Remember that transitions are an opportunity to learn, grow, try out new skills, and cultivate new relationships.

The question is not which one is best, but which one is best for *you*? The assessment you took helps identify your career development style based on your personality. This isn't to say that the style you scored highest in is the style you should adopt–only that it is the style that will probably come most naturally to you. That doesn't mean that a job jumper won't quickly turn into a traditionalist if he or she happens to jump into the perfect job or that an opportunist won't suddenly uncover a deep-seated interest in photography that consumes his or her leisure time, turning him or her into a catalyst. Circumstances change, and our personal preferences, goals, values, and interests change alongside them. The key to successfully managing your career is to fully understand where you are right now, your current aspirations, and the best way to fill them. Knowing your preferred career development style is a first step. Many more are yet to come.

# Tying It All Together

Change happens to all of us, and we all adapt to it differently. Transitions force us to develop and refine our ability to adapt and evolve personally and professionally. The purpose of this chapter was to help you better understand your current (or future) career transition and ways you might handle it.

Being a master of change requires you to be flexible and willing to experiment and explore new ways of doing things. Now that you have learned more about how you react to career transitions, you are ready to work your way through your own transition step by step. The chapters that follow will help you define your career, learn more about your ideal job, and find and succeed in that job.

Remember to complete all the assessments honestly. The key to developing a successful career is knowing who you are, where you stand, and where you want to end up. Then, it's just a matter of walking the path you forge for yourself.

# CHAPTER 2

# Meeting Your Needs

*"A musician must make music, an artist must paint, a poet must write, if he is to be ultimately at peace with himself."*
*–Abraham Maslow*

A career transition is an opportunity, a chance to find greater satisfaction elsewhere. Often, people know they are ready for such a transition, but they can't tell you why. They don't feel fulfilled, but they can't pinpoint the source of their dissatisfaction. Other people do know what they need and eagerly wait for the right opportunity to come along.

Take Rick, for example. Rick and I both worked as career counselors, helping unemployed steel mill workers in Pittsburgh find jobs. I loved this job. Rick, on the other hand, earned a reputation as a bad employee. He came in late for work, was not motivated to help his clients, and kept telling me that he was not living up to his potential. He wanted to be outdoors more, not sitting behind a desk all day. He also said that he needed to be selling something so that he could "keep score."

Then, fate stepped in. One of our job developers was injured and needed to miss two weeks of work. Job developers are staff who go out into the city and ask employers if they would consider hiring any of the clients registered with a government agency. Seeing an opportunity to try something new, Rick volunteered.

This seemed to transform him. He loved going out and getting employers to hire our clients. He made it a game and saw it as a personal challenge. He discovered a natural talent for sales. He felt like he could use his full potential, and people at the agency praised his efforts. I wondered how the same person could completely shift his motivation within two weeks, working with the same organization and making the same amount of money. The answer was simple: He found a job that met more of his needs. The agency rewarded Rick by hiring him as a full-time job developer.

# Satisfaction, Motivation, and Needs

Job satisfaction describes how content you are with your job. It is not the same as motivation, but the two are clearly linked. Motivation is the inner desire to take action. When you feel motivated, you do what needs to be done because you want to, not simply because you have to. Motivation stems from self-interest. Therefore, finding something that satisfies as many of your desires as possible is the first step in increasing your level of motivation.

We all have inner drives or impulses that motivate us. For career success, it is important that you understand how your drives propel you to do what you do. These inner drives are called needs, and like all people, you are driven to satisfy various needs on the job, at home, at school, or in your community.

While we all have needs, we seek to fulfill them in different ways and to different degrees. Some people must concentrate on fulfilling basic needs like food and clothing, whereas others focus on higher-level needs like nurturing relationships or engaging in lifelong learning. Knowing what your specific needs are—and the various ways you try to satisfy them—is an important step in your career development.

# Maslow's Theory of Motivation

Many years ago, psychologist Abraham Maslow developed a theory that emphasized the influence of needs on our behavior. He theorized that as needs emerge in us, they determine our motivations and, by consequence, our actions. An unsatisfied need for companionship, for example, can motivate us to ask someone out on a date, call a friend up for dinner, chat online, or adopt a puppy. More to the point, a job that doesn't satisfy one or more of your needs can also prompt you to take action, such as quitting it in order to look for another one (and that emerging need for a new job will prompt more actions, such as reading the want ads or buying a book full of career quizzes). Maslow felt that everything we do is done to satisfy some inner need and that by truly understanding our needs, we can truly understand our behaviors.

We are all constantly struggling to meet our inner needs, and we meet many of them by the work we do. Thank goodness we all have only five basic categories of needs to meet:

- **Physiological Needs:** The need for food, air, drink, sleep, and sex. These needs are usually the most powerful of all human needs. They can block out or overpower all other needs if they are not met. If we don't satisfy them, our lives could be in danger.

- **Safety and Security Needs:** The need to live in a relatively safe and stable environment and the need to feel psychologically secure. Such needs might include the need for structure, order, and limits in your life. In addition, they include the need to live free from fear, chaos, and anxiety. Someone choosing between two job offers might take the one that comes with a matching 401(k) to meet this need.

- **Love and Belonging Needs:** The need to have close relationships with others and feel a part of groups such as family, community, or friends. While this need is often satisfied by intimate relationships with other people or belonging to a variety of social groups, a person's job or career can also satisfy his or her sense of belonging. Getting along with your coworkers is one thing, but being part of a close-knit team with a common purpose can be one of the most rewarding aspects of a career.

- **Esteem Needs:** Our need for feelings of worth and adequacy. We often satisfy self-esteem needs through individual achievement and by garnering respect from others, usually in the form of recognition, status, and fame. If needs at this level are not met, people often feel helpless and inferior. For many of us, our career is the primary contributor to our self-esteem. It is often through our work that we receive the most recognition. Likewise, a lack of recognition at work is one sign that it's time to reevaluate your career path.

> **NOTE**
>
> At any given time, you are being motivated by your lowest unsatisfied need. You work until that need becomes reasonably well satisfied before moving on to additional needs.

- **Self-Actualization Needs:** Self-actualization refers to the realization and fulfillment of one's potential. People who can't make the most of their abilities often become discontented and restless. Of course, self-actualization is different for all people. For one, being an excellent parent may be the goal; for another, political activism in the community is key; for others, it might be becoming a good athlete, painter, or business executive. We can achieve self-actualization through a variety of life roles, of course, not just through our career. But our careers often provide the best potential for reaching self-actualization–provided we take them in the right direction.

Maslow arranged these needs in a hierarchy from the most potent needs at the bottom to the least potent needs at the top.

**Self-Actualization:** Your desire for creativity and maximizing your full potential.

**Esteem:** Your desire for respect, divided into self-esteem and esteem for others.

**Love and Belonging:** Various social needs, including your desire for love, companionship, and friendship.

**Safety and Security:** Your need to be safe and secure.

**Physiological:**
Your biological needs: water, food, rest, sex, and air.

You spend most of your life trying to find work and leisure activities to satisfy your needs. As soon as you satisfy one need, however, another immediately takes its place. Maslow believed that we all constantly strive to meet needs in order to actualize our full potential–to reach the top of the pyramid.

# The Career Needs Inventory

The following assessment helps you identify your needs and the extent to which your career does or can fulfill them. Keep in mind that no career–no matter how wonderful–can satisfy every need. If it did, we would never leave work. However, by better defining your needs, you can more easily adapt your current job to meet as many of them as possible–or find a job that will.

---

### ASSESSING THE PRESENT AND PLANNING FOR THE FUTURE

Assessments can be either diagnostic (designed to describe present behavior) or prognostic (designed to predict future behavior). Some of the assessments in this book (like the one that follows) are diagnostic in nature. They seek to describe your career behaviors so that you can enhance what works and change what doesn't. Other assessments are essentially predictive in nature, such as the assessments in Part II, which are designed to predict future job satisfaction based on personal characteristics.

Please read each statement carefully. Using the following scale, circle the number that best describes how important each item is in your career.

| | Very Important | Important | Somewhat Important | Not Important |
|---|---|---|---|---|
| **I currently need work...** | | | | |
| 1. that allows me to pay the bills | 4 | 3 | 2 | 1 |
| 2. that is physically comfortable to perform | 4 | 3 | 2 | 1 |
| 3. that I can do without too much pressure | 4 | 3 | 2 | 1 |
| 4. that will allow me to buy a house or pay the rent | 4 | 3 | 2 | 1 |
| 5. that allows me to engage in my favorite leisure activities | 4 | 3 | 2 | 1 |
| 6. that does not cut into my family time too much | 4 | 3 | 2 | 1 |
| 7. that provides time for lunch and breaks during the day | 4 | 3 | 2 | 1 |
| 8. that helps me feed my family | 4 | 3 | 2 | 1 |
| **I. Total: _____** | | | | |
| **I currently need work...** | | | | |
| 9. that allows me to make lots of money | 4 | 3 | 2 | 1 |
| 10. that provides me with good benefits, such as health insurance | 4 | 3 | 2 | 1 |
| 11. where I am not afraid of losing my job if I make a mistake | 4 | 3 | 2 | 1 |
| 12. in which I will not be harmed or injured | 4 | 3 | 2 | 1 |
| 13. where I know what is expected of me | 4 | 3 | 2 | 1 |
| 14. that will still be in demand in the future | 4 | 3 | 2 | 1 |
| 15. that has regularly scheduled hours | 4 | 3 | 2 | 1 |
| 16. that offers a good retirement plan | 4 | 3 | 2 | 1 |
| **II. Total: _____** | | | | |
| **I currently need work...** | | | | |
| 17. that allows me to be an effective team member | 4 | 3 | 2 | 1 |
| 18. where I like my coworkers | 4 | 3 | 2 | 1 |
| 19. in which I am supported and guided by others | 4 | 3 | 2 | 1 |
| 20. where I make a valuable contribution to society | 4 | 3 | 2 | 1 |
| 21. where I get plenty of contact with other people | 4 | 3 | 2 | 1 |
| 22. where I am mentored by someone | 4 | 3 | 2 | 1 |
| 23. where I can help and support others | 4 | 3 | 2 | 1 |
| 24. where I am accepted by coworkers | 4 | 3 | 2 | 1 |
| **III. Total: _____** | | | | |

*(continued)*

*(continued)*

| | Very Important | Important | Somewhat Important | Not Important |
|---|---|---|---|---|
| **I currently need work...** | | | | |
| 25. in which I am adequately paid for my performance | 4 | 3 | 2 | 1 |
| 26. where my talents are appreciated | 4 | 3 | 2 | 1 |
| 27. that makes me feel proud | 4 | 3 | 2 | 1 |
| 28. where I am acknowledged for my achievements | 4 | 3 | 2 | 1 |
| 29. where I control my own destiny | 4 | 3 | 2 | 1 |
| 30. that my colleagues, family, and friends can respect | 4 | 3 | 2 | 1 |
| 31. in which I can receive promotions for my performance | 4 | 3 | 2 | 1 |
| 32. in which I feel like I make a significant contribution | 4 | 3 | 2 | 1 |
| **IV. Total:** _____ | | | | |
| **I currently need work...** | | | | |
| 33. that allows me to grow personally | 4 | 3 | 2 | 1 |
| 34. that allows me to contribute to a worthwhile cause | 4 | 3 | 2 | 1 |
| 35. that allows me to fully use my skills and abilities | 4 | 3 | 2 | 1 |
| 36. that is meaningful to me | 4 | 3 | 2 | 1 |
| 37. that helps me reach my ultimate career goals | 4 | 3 | 2 | 1 |
| 38. through which I can achieve my full potential | 4 | 3 | 2 | 1 |
| 39. that requires a great deal of creativity | 4 | 3 | 2 | 1 |
| 40. in which I am continually learning new things | 4 | 3 | 2 | 1 |
| **V. Total:** _____ | | | | |

# Scoring

Add up the scores you circled for each section. Put each total on the appropriate line at the end of each section. For each section, you will have a total ranging from 8 to 32. Then, transfer your totals to the spaces below:

I. **Physiological Needs:** _____     II. **Safety and Security Needs:** _____

III. **Belonging and Love Needs:** _____     IV. **Esteem Needs:** _____

V. **Self-Actualization Needs:** _____

A score from 8—15 on any scale is low and indicates that the work you desire does not necessarily have to meet this particular set of needs. For example, if you scored low on the Belonging and Love Needs scale, this probably means that you do not need to develop strong bonds with your coworkers (most likely because you are having those needs met elsewhere–through relationships with family or friends, for example).

By contrast, a score from 25—32 on any scale is high and indicates that your work should definitely meet this particular set of needs in order to be satisfying. For example, if you scored high on the Esteem Needs scale, this probably means you will not be happy at work unless you feel confident in the work you do and earn the respect of your coworkers and colleagues.

# Meeting Your Needs

The fact that you are reading this book suggests that you feel the need to improve your career situation to better meet your needs. You should first identify your highest score; that will tell you which of the five need levels is most important to you. You should then do everything you can to reach that level.

The following exercises will help you explore your career needs at each level. Concentrate on those needs that are most important to you, but don't neglect the others. After all, the ultimate goal is to have *all* your needs met in both your career and your life.

> **NOTE**
>
> Lower scores do not mean that those needs are not important. It simply means that those needs are not as prominent for you, that you are meeting them elsewhere, or that you are willing to sacrifice them to meet greater needs.

## *The Bare Necessities: Physiological Needs*

Your first level of needs is physiological and includes the need for money for basic life essentials: food, physical comfort, a place to live, work without much stress, and work that allows you to continue to engage in leisure activities. These needs tend to be the most powerful of all human needs; when they are unfulfilled, you experience an urgent motivation to satisfy them.

| EXERCISE |
| --- |
| Is your current job providing you with enough income to meet your basic needs? What basic needs are not being met? |

| MONEY DOESN'T EQUAL HAPPINESS |
|---|
| Don't dwell on money as the "end all" of needs satisfaction. At all the needs levels, money is simply a means to an end. At the higher levels of Maslow's pyramid, money becomes less important and sometimes gets in the way. In fact, studies have shown that once you have enough to be comfortable, happiness is more a matter of attitude and interests and less a matter of income. In fact, some theorists have even suggested a dollar amount for the happiness equation: $40,000. Making any more than that per year, they say, is no more likely to make you happy than anything else is. |

There is, of course, a difference between wants and needs. Wants are those things that you desire but that are not critical to advancing to the next stage of career fulfillment. For example, you might want two cars and a house with four bedrooms and three baths. Maslow would say that these are wants because they are not necessary. (Of course, if you have a family of six or more, you could make an argument to the contrary.) This need level is more concerned with basic day-to-day living and less concerned with long-term financial security or accumulating wealth and property. In the following exercise, try to differentiate between your wants and your needs. This will help you focus on what's most important to you as you develop your career.

| EXERCISE |
|---|

| Things I Want | Things I Need |
|---|---|
| _____ | _____ |
| _____ | _____ |
| _____ | _____ |
| _____ | _____ |

Keep in mind that a job that does not fulfill your needs at this first level is ultimately not doing its job. At the most basic level, most of us work to "make a living," a phrase that has much more to do with survival (the bottom of Maslow's pyramid) than self-actualization (the top). If you find that your physiological needs are your most important, then perhaps a safer, less stressful, or better-paying job is the first step toward moving up the hierarchy and realizing your larger goals.

## No Guarantees in Life: Safety and Security Needs

This level represents our need to live free from fear, illness, injury, chaos, and anxiety–no small concerns in the face of rising health care costs and the uncertain future of Social Security. On the job, the need for safety and security relates to many employees' concern for a more stable workplace. The workplace of the new millennium is unpredictable. Many companies have downsized, restructured, outsourced work to independent contractors and foreign countries, and undergone radical technological changes. Globalization continues to present employees with competitive challenges and loss of employment. It is estimated that up to three million jobs are lost each year due to the increased exporting of goods from other countries.

Even the employees who keep their jobs experience changes that affect their sense of safety and security. More and more employers are making employees pay a larger percentage of their own health care benefits and providing fewer sick days. When I got my first job, my employer paid 100 percent of my medical expenses. Nowadays, people take jobs with less pay or worse hours for the promise of better health insurance. Safety and security in the workplace are no longer automatic propositions. 401(k)s can dwindle to nothing, housing prices can skyrocket or plummet, and you never know when one company will gobble up another, resulting in a shift in policy or, even worse, in personnel. All these changes call for employees to work with less safety and security than they ever had to in the past.

Because corporations often have no or limited loyalty to their employees, today's workers increasingly show an "every-employee-for-himself-or-herself" mentality. It also forces many employees to begin their own small or home-based businesses or find part-time employment to supplement their full-time work.

In the boxes below, please check the various ways that your current (or previous) job provides you with safety and security:

- ☐ Security from crime
- ☐ Safety from debt
- ☐ Security from injury
- ☐ Stability from chaos
- ☐ Job security in the future

- ☐ Feeling that your family is safe
- ☐ Security of health
- ☐ Security of retirement
- ☐ Steady paycheck

Now, in the boxes below, please check the various ways that your current job threatens (or past jobs have threatened) your safety and security:

- ☐ Job loss due to technology
- ☐ Job loss due to poor performance
- ☐ Job loss due to office politics
- ☐ Forced retirement
- ☐ Organizational shutdown

- ☐ Work sent to another country
- ☐ Health benefits cut
- ☐ Lack of retirement plan
- ☐ Lack of consistent pay increases

Certainly, many of the things that threaten our safety and security are outside our control. Whether it's a new robot, a corporate buyout, or a decision by management to stop offering a 401(k), there are some changes we can do little about. On the other hand, there are many things you *can* do to improve the feeling of security you get from your job. You can improve your performance, work toward a promotion, or negotiate a higher salary so that you can invest more in your own retirement plan, just to name a few. The key is to recognize those things you can change about the job to feel more secure. Of course, when something comes along that threatens your feelings of security, you must be willing to take the necessary action to fulfill that need–even if it means finding a new job.

In the first column below, list some things about your job that threaten your safety and security. Then, in the second column, identify some things you could change about your job to feel more secure.

---

**EXERCISE**

| Current Work Insecurities | How I Could Change My Current Job |
|---|---|
| _____ | _____ |
| _____ | _____ |
| _____ | _____ |
| _____ | _____ |

---

## *People Who Need People: Belonging and Love Needs*

Human beings have a natural motivation to maintain close relationships with others and feel part of a group. Within our careers, we can fulfill this need through relationships with coworkers and through interactions with customers and clients. Although we may not think of ourselves as loving our coworkers (and there may be policies *against* such things where you work), a sense of camaraderie often exists that can help satisfy this need (or a sense of hostility that can keep it from being satisfied).

---

**EXERCISE**

Make a list of the ways your work can help fulfill your needs for belonging and love:

_____

_____

_____

_____

---

Because so much of our sense of belonging stems from our relationships with coworkers and because those relationships depend so heavily on interpersonal skills, it is important for people who have a strong need for belonging and love to develop those skills. In the list that follows, check off anything you could do to improve your interpersonal skills:

- ☐ Develop better listening skills.
- ☐ Develop better conflict-resolution skills.
- ☐ Develop more empathy.
- ☐ Learn how to give constructive feedback.
- ☐ Learn how to cultivate friendships better.
- ☐ Learn to accept people's differences.
- ☐ Learn how to assert yourself when necessary.
- ☐ Learn how to express your feelings better.
- ☐ Learn to develop and maintain trust.
- ☐ Learn how to make small talk and be more sociable.

In our highly mobile, often cubicled, and individualistic workplace, many people become frustrated trying to meet these needs. Many people do so by working on team projects or developing friendships with coworkers. Find hobbies or leisure interests that you share with coworkers and then use these activities as a way to get to know them better. Take time during your day to stop and chat with coworkers, and you'll find that they will return the favor.

Of course, you may not want to develop friendships with your coworkers. While our careers can certainly help satisfy our need for belonging and love, we usually look to relationships outside of work for that purpose. It can become difficult to keep your work role separate from the rest of your life.

— **N O T E** —

When you do make the effort to get to know your coworkers, they can go a long way toward fulfilling your need to belong.

Sometimes, it isn't a question of how your job can satisfy your need for belonging and love but how it can *keep* you from fulfilling that need. The two working parents who fear they don't spend enough time with their children, the husband who feels his wife is away on business too often, or the person who can't relax around friends because she thinks about work are all examples of how work can impact relationships and affect how well our needs are met.

## EXERCISE

What impact does your work have on your relationships outside of work—with your family, friends, or significant other, for example?

_____

_____

_____

_____

---

**EXERCISE**

What are some ways you can improve this situation (more vacation time, part-time work, not taking work home, etc.)?

_____

_____

_____

_____

---

## Good Enough, Smart Enough, and People Like Me: Esteem Needs

Esteem needs drive us to obtain a feeling of worth, a good reputation, and confidence in the use of our abilities. You can satisfy such needs through achievement and the knowledge that you are providing a good service, helping others, or doing your job better than other people. A salesperson may find self-esteem in meeting her sales goals for the month, whereas a nurse may maintain his self-esteem by helping a patient beat cancer. Thus, self-esteem is largely determined by and different for each individual. The teacher who helps a student learn to read, the surgeon with a 97 percent success rate, or the roofer who develops a reputation for quality work all find their own path to increased self-esteem.

---

**EXERCISE**

In the space below, list three things that you have done in your life that you are most proud of. They do not have to be work related.

_____

_____

_____

---

Feeling good about ourselves is important, but the feeling often doesn't come from within. We all need respect from others—often in the form of recognition, prestige, status, and fame. These needs motivate us to do our best in return for some kind of acknowledgment from the outside world. This can be as simple as a pat on the back or as ambitious as winning a Nobel Prize. Employee-of-the- Month certificates, private parking spaces, merit raises, honorary degrees, or a simple compliment from a coworker in passing all contribute to fulfilling this need. When such needs are not met, people often feel helpless and inferior, uncertain of their worth.

Self-esteem is the way you feel about yourself and your perception of your worth. People with high self-esteem view themselves as equal to others. They do not think that they are perfect, but they recognize their limitations and continually strive to grow and improve. I have known many people who have a high need for self-esteem and found themselves in a job where they did not respect the work they did or feel as if others respected them. In most of these situations, the people had to look for new jobs where they could feel good about themselves and their work.

In the boxes below, check the various ways that your work is recognized by your supervisors, coworkers, customers, and/or clients:

- ☐ Bonuses
- ☐ Certificates
- ☐ Comment cards
- ☐ Company products or discounts
- ☐ Company stock
- ☐ Gift cards
- ☐ Great salary
- ☐ Mention in the company newsletter
- ☐ Merit raises

- ☐ Notes from others
- ☐ Promotions
- ☐ Recommendations
- ☐ Referrals
- ☐ Time off from work
- ☐ Trophies
- ☐ Verbal praise
- ☐ Other: _____

## EXERCISE

In the space below, list some things you do on the job that make you feel good about yourself:

_____

_____

_____

Now list some things you could do on the job to feel better about yourself:

_____

_____

_____

# Answering the Call: Self-Actualization

Self-actualization is the realization of your full potential—it's you becoming who you were meant to be. If you can't identify and utilize all your abilities and talents, you will likely become discontented and restless. Self-actualization needs motivate you to seek and find meaning and purpose, to fully express your creativity, and to experience and enjoy the beauty in life. Self-actualization expresses itself when you can find a job that you love and that lets you use your talents.

Maslow believed that living at a higher level of needs is healthier and more satisfying than living at lower levels. Most of us wish we had more of our basic needs met so that we could live a richer life, pursue higher goals, or simply grow more as individuals. But it isn't easy. The pyramid is steep and slippery in spots. Maslow suggested that it can be very difficult for people to reach and maintain a high level of self-actualization. Those who do begin by knowing which needs motivate them the most; by having intimate knowledge of their interests, skills, personality, and values; and then finding a way to incorporate these into their careers.

> **NOTE**
>
> Self-actualization needs are difficult to meet because they are not as powerful. If you don't have friends, car insurance, or a roof over your head, you probably have more urgent needs to attend to than expressing your creativity.

No job will likely satisfy you all the time, of course. Instead, self-actualization motivates you to seek out "peak" experiences in which you can fully grow and let your inner nature express itself freely. Peak experience moments, according to Maslow, are not only a person's happiest and most thrilling moments, but also a person's healthiest moments–moments of great fulfillment, maturity, and individuation.

---

### EXERCISE

In the space below, describe any "peak" experiences you've had in your career:

_____

_____

_____

Describe how your job allows you to use all your talents and abilities. If it does not, which ones do you not use on the job? What kind of work could you do that would help you make the most of your talents?

_____

_____

_____

---

Maslow felt that people could achieve self-actualization by doing the following:

- Find interests that you can devote yourself to fully.

- Take responsibility for your life and career.

- Dare to be your own person. Don't worry so much about what other people say and think.

- Realize your potential. Find ways to perfect your talents and abilities.

- Live for "peak experiences." Peak experiences are moments of self-actualization when you are truly using all your potential.

Consider how you can begin to incorporate some or all of these into your career and your life.

Self-actualizing people are usually involved in a cause outside of themselves–a calling or vocation. Often, they devote their lives and their work to the pursuit of higher values, such as truth, goodness, beauty, wholeness, transcendence, justice, or simplicity. Maslow suggested that such a pursuit represented the meaning of life for most people.

Maslow contends that many people are "called" to their occupations, much like a spiritual leader feels "called" to do the work he or she does. John Schuster, in his book *Answering Your Call*, says that callings are invitations from life to serve–to activate your will toward a cause worthy of you and humankind. He likes to think of callings as a purpose with a voice–opportunities to live a life that fully uses your innate talents and adds some lasting value to the world. As Schuster says, callings "turn insurance policy peddlers into advisors of needed financial security, grocery store employees into health and nutrition suppliers, doctors into healers, secretaries into stewards, businesspeople into entrepreneurs, bureaucrats into civil servants, writers into dream weavers, and parents into co-creators of life."

How can you identify your calling? Answering the following questions will get you started:

- What activities do you engage in and lose track of time?

- What do you do that is not important to anyone else but yourself?

- What are you doing when you feel peace and serenity?

- What do you do that just seems to come naturally?

- What do you do that leaves you feeling energized instead of drained?

---

**EXERCISE**

In the space below, describe how your work is your calling or, if it is not, what kind of job you feel might be your calling:

_____

_____

_____

---

Remember that self-actualization is not about being famous, making millions, or owning a château on the French Riviera. It's not even about being popular or well loved. Self-actualization is about making the most of your abilities and being the best that you possibly can. The form that self-actualization takes differs for everyone. Perhaps you cannot answer this question until you have read more of this book. Maybe the answer changes. (We can, in fact, have more than one calling.) Or the answer might just come to you in time.

For now, simply think about what you are interested in that seems greater than yourself. For some people, it might be helping or serving others, establishing a business, or researching cures for diseases. It might be something no one has even thought of yet. But whatever it is, it will be uniquely yours because it will involve you realizing your full potential.

## Meeting Your Needs at Work

Whether it's the need to put food on our tables or roofs over our heads or the higher need to become the best person we can, there is no question that our jobs play a major role in our need fulfillment. The vast majority, at the very minimum, must work in order to have their basic needs met. (Those who aren't paid for the work they do undoubtedly have other needs being fulfilled.)

Most of us spend a third of our waking hours at work–that's a lot of time for pyramid climbing.

> **— NOTE —**
>
> More often than not, your needs will overlap. Therefore, a job that is a great match for your interests, personality, and skills will probably allow you to meet many of your needs.

And for those whose jobs don't satisfy their needs, it feels like time wasted. Perhaps that's why many executives quit their jobs and put away their business suits to go teach or volunteer; certainly, lower levels can be satisfied by a well-paying job, but if you don't like what you do or who you work with, or if the work doesn't help you grow or give you a feeling of accomplishment, odds are you could get stuck on the lower levels of the pyramid and feel unfulfilled.

Now that you've had the chance to identify which needs are most important to you and which are being met or not met, you should have a better sense of where you stand. Likewise, if you completed some of the exercises above, you should have a better idea of how well your work fulfills your needs.

Complete the exercise below to summarize what you've learned about yourself in this chapter. In the first column, list those needs being met through your work (or that were met at your previous job). Then, in the second column, list the needs that you have that are not being met at work.

| EXERCISE | |
|---|---|
| **Needs Being Met** | **Needs Not Being Met** |
| _____ | _____ |
| _____ | _____ |
| _____ | _____ |
| _____ | _____ |
| _____ | _____ |

What can you do to ensure that more of your needs are met through your work? In the spaces below, list your goals for having more of your needs met and then list some strategies you will use to meet those goals. For example, if your goal is to "Start being more creative at work," then a strategy would be to "Ask my supervisor for more challenging tasks or projects."

---

**EXERCISE**

Goal: _____

Strategies for attaining that goal:

_____

_____

Goal: _____

Strategies for attaining that goal:

_____

_____

Goal: _____

Strategies for attaining that goal:

_____

_____

---

# Meeting Needs in Other Life Roles

Although many of us would like our career to fill all or most of our needs, such expectations are unrealistic. Truthfully, we all take on several roles in life, and each of them contributes to our need for fulfillment. Sometimes, roles combine to fill one need, like a person receiving praise from both a coworker and a family member to contribute to her self-esteem. But roles often conflict, as one role meets a need at the expense of another. Imagine someone who quits a secure job in order to start his own business. Such a move risks satisfying the need for safety and security for both him and his family, but it could go a long way toward helping him reach self-actualization.

It is important to find a job and develop a career that will meet as many of your needs as possible. But it is equally important to recognize the limitations your career has to meet all of them and to supplement them by also letting your other life roles satisfy needs.

---

**EXERCISE**

For each life role below that applies to you (and not all of them will), list the needs that role fulfills for you. Compare that list to your list of needs not being met at work. Hopefully, between work and your other life roles, all your needs are being met. If not, you need to concentrate on finding new ways to meet them as you develop your career.

**Other Life Roles**                    **Needs Being Met by That Role**

Student        _____

Parent         _____

Child          _____

Citizen        _____

Spouse         _____

Friend         _____

Volunteer      _____

Other          _____

---

# Tying It All Together

Our needs drive us. They dictate our actions and behaviors. They change our plans and cause us to draw up new ones. They help us define our goals and then push us to reach them. A successful career is one that seeks to satisfy all your needs by pushing you to realize your full potential. Those needs are different for each of us, so no single career path works for everyone. The key is to develop a path that is right for you—one that gives you room to grow and satisfy higher needs until you find your "calling."

By identifying and understanding the needs that motivate you most in your work, you have taken the next step toward redefining your career path so that it leads to personal success. The next chapter will explore one potential—and increasingly common—path to fulfilling those needs: entrepreneurship.

# CHAPTER 3

# Being the Boss

*"The most successful entrepreneurs know that the greatest knowledge is self-knowledge. They're not necessarily blessed with a higher intellect or more charisma than others, but they understand how to make the best of their talents and how to manage or compensate for their weaknesses."*
*–Bill Wagner,* The Entrepreneur Next Door

Janice wakes up to find that she hadn't set her alarm clock and it's already a quarter after eight. For most of us, this would be a problem–15 minutes late for work and we haven't even showered yet. But Janice isn't concerned. She figures she'll just go to work in her pajamas. She'll work for a few hours, and then go for a jog and shower afterward. Her boss thinks this is a splendid idea. After all, she's an independent Web designer working from her own home. She is her own boss.

One possible path to fulfilling the needs you identified in the last chapter could be self-employment. Recent research suggests that nearly half of all Americans have considered self-employment, with nearly 700,000 Americans starting new businesses each year. Of course, the research also suggests that many of these ventures will shut down after only one year.

> **NOTE**
>
> The benefits of self-employment are obvious, but so are the risks. One way to alleviate some of that risk is to keep your full-time job and start an entrepreneurial pursuit in your spare time. That way, you can have the security of a paycheck and benefits while pursuing your dreams of self-employment.

In reality, only about 7 percent of Americans are self-employed. Most working Americans feel they can't afford to quit their full-time jobs to start a business. They've heard horror stories about the number of entrepreneurial efforts that fail. They worry about losing the medical benefits that accompany most jobs in this age of rising health care costs. They are afraid of uncertainty.

These are legitimate concerns, and added to them is the simple fact that being self-employed or starting your own business takes a lot of resources and hard work. Yet, nearly 1 in 10 Americans has found a way to make it work, and almost all of them will tell you it is well worth the risk–provided you have the attitude and determination to make a go of it.

# The Truth About Success

In their book *The Millionaire Next Door,* Thomas Stanley and William Danko discuss the factors that make millionaires successful. Their research is the most comprehensive ever conducted on the people who are wealthy in America and how they got that way. Among other things, they discovered the following:

- Self-employed people make up less than 10 percent of the workers in America but account for two-thirds of the millionaires. Three out of four of those who were self-employed considered themselves entrepreneurs; the others were self-employed service providers.

- Usually, millionaires are business people who have lived in the same town for all their adult lives. These people own a small factory, a chain of stores, farms, or a service business.

- Self-employed people are four times more likely to be millionaires than those who work for others.

- The personal characteristics of business owners are more important in predicting their level of wealth than the type of business they own.

Although these millionaires undoubtedly appreciate the financial rewards that come with successful business ventures, most try entrepreneurship because they enjoy the freedom of being their own boss. By working for themselves, they can control their own destiny. Self-employment often fills needs at multiple levels, whether it is the financial rewards, the prestige that comes from being a successful entrepreneur, or the realization of one's full potential as one builds a business from scratch. Of course, this requires a great deal of time and energy, and it's not for everyone.

The purpose of this chapter and the assessment it contains is to help you decide whether self-employment is right for you.

---

**IT IS NEVER TOO LATE!**

The American Association of Retired Persons (AARP) recently released its own study that explored the number of older Americans becoming self-employed. This study shows that older workers are quickly joining the national trend toward self-employment. The interesting fact was that among workers age 50 and older, 16.4 percent are self-employed–much higher than the national average. In addition, one in three of these workers made the transition to self-employment after the age of 50.

---

## *The New Entrepreneur*

Choosing to become an entrepreneur is a major life decision, one that often goes against our upbringing. After all, the American dream is built on the notion that to be successful, you have to work your way up a "corporate ladder." My parents always stressed that career advancement with a large corporation was the way to attain success and happiness. This career path usually means getting as much education as you possibly can, working hard, climbing rung by rung, and having a good attitude about it all.

This path to success has been taught since the time the Puritans first came to this country. This philosophy, based on the idea of a linear career and catering to the organizations that shape careers, has provided the framework for the American values of individual accomplishment, competition, personal responsibility, and success at all costs. However, notions of success are changing, and new breeds of entrepreneurs have emerged, defining success on their own terms.

These new entrepreneurs believe that they can achieve success and fulfill personal needs and dreams by starting entrepreneurial ventures while retaining full-time jobs. Several characteristics prompt these new entrepreneurs to pursue this goal in a society fraught with change:

- **Discontent with 9 to 5:** The new entrepreneurs are not content working for someone else. They demand work that provides more intrinsic rewards, such as an opportunity to be creative, to have fun, to take risks, and to use all their talents. The new entrepreneur resists the idea of simply "making a living"–getting up every morning and going to a job that is not fulfilling or challenging and where most of us have no autonomy or input into the decisions that are made.

- **The myth of job security:** Many of us grew up believing that you go to work for a company, corporation, or government agency and work there until you retire. Our parents raised us to believe that a company is our friend and will take care of us. Yet, we all know that this is just not true in today's work environment. Companies have streamlined operations and forced employees into early retirement–all with an eye on the bottom line. No longer are people guaranteed promotions and pay raises based on their performance at work. For some, work is no longer even available, regardless of education or work experience. In such an insecure world, the risks associated with entrepreneurship suddenly look less risky (or at least equally risky).

- **The growth of small business:** New entrepreneurs know that big business is not where the opportunities are. Most people take jobs in small companies where they find more flexibility and autonomy. Improvements in telecommunications and the explosion of the Internet have made working from home a much more viable alternative. This same technology allows entrepreneurs the opportunity to create their own jobs and businesses without a lot of capital.

- **Being comfortable with change:** New entrepreneurs see change as a necessary ingredient of career development. Since they are not interested in "climbing the corporate ladder," they see no need to stay at one job for an entire career. They look at job hopping as a way of building skills and maintaining their participation in interesting leisure activities. Thus, a job to them is merely a way to make money to support their real interest: the growth of their own business.

> **─── N O T E ───**
>
> Many home-based businesses do not require large amounts of capital. The number of small businesses has doubled over the last 10 years. Corporate buildings that house hundreds or thousands of employees have started to disappear, replaced by e-businesses operated from your neighbor's family room.

Traditionally, entrepreneurship has been defined as the process of starting and developing a new business. In the last decade, entrepreneurship has increasingly been viewed as a mindset or attitude that a person develops about work and freedom. Some of these shifting attitudes about working for yourself versus working for someone else include the following:

## Owning Your Own Business

- You are the owner of your time.

- Financial rewards depend on your efforts.

- Work and leisure are fused together.

- You direct the work.

- You have time for family and friends when you need it.

## Working for Someone Else

- You are at the mercy of an employer.

- Financial rewards are fixed and determined by the employer.

- Leisure comes only when work is done.

- Your supervisor directs the work.

- Time off needs to be scheduled and approved.

# *Doing What You Love*

Have you ever been engaged in a hobby or activity that you enjoyed and thought, "How come I can't do *this* for a living?" Many small and home-based businesses start as an outgrowth of a leisure interest. Take, for instance, the teenager who turns a trading-card collection into a profitable business or the teacher who enjoys painting in her spare time and eventually opens a small art gallery in her home. Our leisure activities are often untapped sources of marketable skills and self-employment possibilities. In fact, most successful entrepreneurs aren't in it for the money but are driven by their passion for the work they do. After all, it was that passion that prompted them to start their own business in the first place.

---

## Making Your Mark

The October 10, 2005, issue of *Forbes* magazine highlighted some of the most successful, influential entrepreneurs. Can you match the person with his entrepreneurial accomplishment?

**Ray Dolby**　　**Ray Tomlinson**　　**Pierre Omidyar**　　**Stanley Hubbard**　　**Robert Rich Sr.**

1. Former computer programmer who started an online auction site in 1995 that allowed consumers to buy and sell everything from Alaskan acreage to vintage haute couture. _____

2. World War II "milk administrator" who invented a soy-based topping that stayed "whippable" even after being frozen. The first to market the homespun miracle of whipped cream in a can, he accumulated profits reaching $2.5 billion. _____

3. Engineer and physicist who made a fortune developing an audio-processing system that eliminates hiss and other background noise from movies and stereo equipment, earning him $1.4 billion. _____

4. Believed that people should have unlimited channel choices while watching television. His first company, U.S. Satellite Broadcasting, was later purchased by DirecTV, helping him to accumulate $1.3 billion. _____

5. In 1971, this MIT graduate wrote a program that allowed one computer to send messages to another computer on the same network, thus creating e-mail. He did not patent the program, however, and missed an opportunity to be a billionaire. _____

*Answers: 1. Pierre Omidyar; 2. Robert Rich Sr.; 3. Ray Dolby; 4. Stanley Hubbard; 5. Ray Tomlinson.*

---

This isn't to say that wannabe entrepreneurs can simply snap their fingers and turn their favorite hobby into million-dollar enterprises. While everyone has something they enjoy, not everyone has the skills to be an entrepreneur. It takes a great deal of perseverance and planning, not to mention a little creativity and a willingness to take risks. But if you are one of the millions who are disenchanted with the prospect of working for someone else, the time, effort, and risks involved might be worth it.

# The Entrepreneurial Readiness Assessment

The following assessment can help you decide whether self-employment is a viable option for you. It contains 50 statements related to the qualities shared by successful entrepreneurs. Read each statement to decide whether the statement describes you. If the statement is true for you, circle the number next to that item under the "True" column. If the statement is false for you, circle the number next to that item under the "False" column.

Do not spend too much time thinking about your responses, and be sure to respond to every statement.

| | True | False |
|---|---|---|
| 1. I often overreact to things | 1 | 2 |
| 2. I persist in the face of challenges | 2 | 1 |
| 3. I can be assertive when necessary | 2 | 1 |
| 4. I need other people around when I am working | 1 | 2 |
| 5. I would not consider myself to be "driven" | 1 | 2 |
| 6. I am well organized | 2 | 1 |
| 7. I am knowledgeable about sales and marketing | 2 | 1 |
| 8. I am good at multitasking | 2 | 1 |
| 9. I am not a good writer | 1 | 2 |
| 10. I become frustrated easily | 1 | 2 |
| 11. I am creative | 2 | 1 |
| 12. I am a risk-taker | 2 | 1 |
| 13. I often do not trust my own instincts | 1 | 2 |
| 14. I like to work independently | 2 | 1 |
| 15. I am not very optimistic | 1 | 2 |
| 16. I do not want to punch a time clock | 2 | 1 |
| 17. I am not very competitive | 1 | 2 |
| 18. I will work until the job is complete to my satisfaction | 2 | 1 |
| 19. I have trouble staying on schedule | 1 | 2 |
| 20. I am a self-starter | 2 | 1 |
| 21. I embrace change | 2 | 1 |
| 22. I have difficulty making decisions | 1 | 2 |
| 23. I think business opportunities are everywhere | 2 | 1 |
| 24. I am a procrastinator | 1 | 2 |
| 25. I am results oriented | 2 | 1 |

| | True | False |
|---|---|---|
| 26. I am confident in my abilities | 2 | 1 |
| 27. I have trouble generating ideas | 1 | 2 |
| 28. I hate to be bogged down with details | 1 | 2 |
| 29. I am a visionary thinker | 2 | 1 |
| 30. I would not be comfortable if I did not receive a regular paycheck | 1 | 2 |
| 31. I am thorough and attentive to details | 2 | 1 |
| 32. I have many ideas for businesses I could start | 2 | 1 |
| 33. I have trouble meeting deadlines | 1 | 2 |
| 34. I am easily distracted | 1 | 2 |
| 35. I do not mind working long hours | 2 | 1 |
| 36. I know what a business plan is | 2 | 1 |
| 37. I am a charismatic person | 2 | 1 |
| 38. I am not afraid to make sacrifices | 2 | 1 |
| 39. I like to set clear goals for myself | 2 | 1 |
| 40. I am worried about going into debt | 1 | 2 |
| 41. I prefer to be told what to do | 1 | 2 |
| 42. I am impatient | 1 | 2 |
| 43. I am always thinking about ways to improve things | 2 | 1 |
| 44. I like to solve complex problems | 2 | 1 |
| 45. I am not very good at math | 1 | 2 |
| 46. I tend to blame others when something goes wrong | 1 | 2 |
| 47. I understand the difference between a failure and a setback | 2 | 1 |
| 48. I have been called stubborn by people who know me | 2 | 1 |
| 49. I am willing to commit my savings to a new enterprise | 2 | 1 |
| 50. I do not like managing other people | 1 | 2 |

## *Scoring*

Total the numbers you circled for all the statements. You will get a score from 50 to 100. Write that number in the space below.

**Total:** _____

# The Makings of an Entrepreneur

No assessment, no matter how involved, can tell you for certain whether you will succeed as an entrepreneur. All it can do is give you a sense of where you stand in relation to those who have successfully become self-employed. Even having all the qualities of an entrepreneur doesn't guarantee success. It does, however, provide a starting point–a way to gauge where you stand with regard to self-employment and how much work it would take.

Given the potential risks involved, it is important to know your strengths and weaknesses before you pursue any self-employment options. If you scored in the low or average range on the preceding assessment (any score below 84), you may want to carefully reconsider your options. People with low scores (50—66) should especially talk with family, friends, and professionals before quitting their day jobs. While there are very few barriers that you can't overcome (you can always learn what a business plan is, improve your math skills, or work on your time management), it is arguable that some people's personalities simply aren't suited for self-employment. For example, if you are uncomfortable taking risks; prefer to be told what to do; and don't have one single idea for something you could create, sell, or improve, then self-employment is probably not for you. (Of course, if you are that person, you probably knew that long before you read this chapter.)

If, on the other hand, you scored in the high range (84—100) or feel you have what it takes to start your own business, then it is important to explore your options and begin making plans. The remainder of this chapter (and the rest of this book) can help.

## *The Self-Employment Dream*

If you decide to become self-employed, you should feel passionate about the work you will do. When considering your options, don't limit your thinking. Suppose that you are good at and enjoy gardening. Businesses related to gardening might include such things as opening a lawn and tree service, a greenhouse, a flower shop, a landscaping service, a landscape design service, an orchard, or a Christmas tree farm.

---

**EXERCISE**

Answering the following questions might help you identify some self-employment possibilities:

1. As a child, what did you dream of doing when you grew up?

   _____

   _____

   _____

2.  What activities have brought you the most satisfaction over the last five years?

    _____

    _____

    _____

3.  What do you think you are better at than most people? What do other people say you are good at?

    _____

    _____

    _____

Your answers to these questions will give you valuable insight into the best type of business ventures to pursue.

## A COMMITMENT TO SUCCESS

Entrepreneurial endeavors are not without their disadvantages. Other than the obvious monetary costs, you can expect a variety of personal costs. You should be prepared, at the very least, to make the following commitments:

- **Working steadily:** Self-employed individuals must have self-discipline and a willingness to put in the hours needed to succeed. While you can set your own hours, you must be willing to work without someone standing over you telling you what needs to be done and when. It's important to stay focused and have a healthy work ethic.

- **Working alone:** Home-based business owners must be especially willing to sacrifice "people" contact. This isn't to say that entrepreneurs are completely isolated–only that it can be harder to fill social needs through your work when there isn't someone in a cubicle next to you.

- **Maintaining your professionalism:** Your professionalism will pay off for you in terms of customer satisfaction. Nothing hurts a small business more than being inconsiderate and rude to its customers. This is especially true for the home-based business owner who must rely on word-of-mouth advertising to gain even more business.

- **Paying your own benefits:** You will probably have to purchase your own health insurance and start your own retirement plan. Many home-based business owners pay into individual retirement accounts (IRAs), and most insurance companies can offer individual health insurance. Still, with the rising cost of health insurance and the questionable future of Social Security, these are no small sacrifices.

*(continued)*

*(continued)*

> - **Trusting your intuition:** You must be willing to trust that your ideas are good and that other people will also think so. You must believe in yourself and be willing to follow your instincts.
> - **Being willing to live with a certain amount of uncertainty:** Unlike a traditional job in which you receive a check regularly, the amount of money you make in your own business will largely depend on the number of people who express interest in your service or product. Also, don't forget that a great deal of the money you make will need to be reinvested back into the business.

There are ideas for self-employment all around you. For example, I once counseled an unemployed welder named Joe who told me that several months ago, he blacktopped his driveway. Soon, an impressed neighbor asked how much Joe would charge to do his. Because he worked fast and did a great job, word got around. Today, Joe has his own home-based blacktopping business.

Many people begin their own business by working directly from their homes. This is an excellent way to test the self-employment waters without drowning in the risky seas of full-fledged entrepreneurship. By working from your living room, you eliminate many expenses associated with traditional businesses. There are no lengthy, gas-guzzling commutes, no lunches out, and no extra rent or utility bills for the office. Home-based businesses are more popular than ever, in part because new technology makes it even easier to market and sell your ideas, products, and services to interested parties and customers.

Just be sure to choose a business based on your interests. One reason that many home-based businesses fail is that people are more concerned with what they think will earn them the most money rather than what they are actually skilled at or would enjoy doing. Just think about all the needs you identified in the previous chapters. Self-employment is not worth the risk if it doesn't bring you closer to meeting more of those needs than a typical nine-to-fiver.

## *Types of Home-Based and Small Businesses*

Of course, not every occupation translates well into a home-based business. Surgeon comes to mind. So does firefighter (most garages simply won't hold the truck). Running a bed and breakfast in your home is possible, if it's big enough, but I wouldn't recommend turning your dining room into a full-service bar. Truthfully, some careers are better suited to self-employment than others. Here are some suggestions categorized by the type of business:

> **NOTE**
>
> Keep a running list of possible business ideas in a small notebook that you carry with you. Constantly think about new ideas and new ways of doing things. Think about what is needed in your town or community or goods and services that you could improve on.

- **Service businesses:** Service businesses are the fastest-growing type of home-based business. In this type of business, you perform a personal service for people for a fee—usually something that customers cannot do or prefer not to do themselves. Examples of this type of business include small engine repair, painting houses, counseling, day care, lawn care, accounting, maid or house-cleaning services, home repair, photography, and pet-sitting.

- **Product businesses:** In this type of business, you make and sell products to others for a profit. Product-based self-employment often starts as an outgrowth of a hobby or leisure activity and begins with an idea for a product that is not readily available on the market. For these types of businesses, it is important to have a clearly defined market and the ability to produce the product(s) cost-effectively. It also helps if you can produce something that is unique or appeals to a niche market. Common products include handmade toys, paintings, software, furniture, and pottery.

- **Information businesses:** In this type of business, computer-based services are generally offered from the home. Computer-based home businesses encompass a wide range of services, including desktop publishing, Web design, word processing, paralegal services, information brokering, bookkeeping, editing, and technical writing.

---

## EXERCISE

In the spaces below, brainstorm possible self-employment options that you would like to try. What kinds of products can you make or sell? What skills or services can you offer? What makes your product or service different from everything else on the market?

Type of business: _____

What product or service would you sell? _____

How is what you have to offer different from what is currently on the market?

_____

_____

Type of business: _____

What product or service would you sell? _____

How is what you have to offer different from what is currently on the market?

_____

_____

Type of business: _____

What product or service would you sell? _____

How is what you have to offer different from what is currently on the market?

_____

_____

*(continued)*

*(continued)*

Now think about which one of these self-employment options is most realistically attainable and will provide you with the greatest satisfaction. Write it here, along with why you think it is the best option:

_____

_____

_____

To help crystallize your thinking, use the space below to write a complete description of your current or proposed business. Pretend that you are talking to a loan officer about obtaining a small-business loan.

_____

_____

_____

_____

_____

## *Getting Started*

While every good business starts with a good idea, that idea alone won't get you very far (unless you can patent it and sell it to someone for a cool million). The truth is, most people who are self-employed work just as hard, if not harder, than people who aren't. They just do it on their own terms. While the "to-do" lists of becoming self-employed vary considerably, the following checklist can give you some idea of what's involved as well as serve as a reminder of where you stand and what you still need to accomplish.

### Business Readiness Checklist

Check off the following tasks you have completed that relate to starting your own business. The items are not in any particular order.

|  | Completed | In Progress | Yet to Start |
|---|---|---|---|
| Identify your business | ☐ | ☐ | ☐ |
| Identify your market | ☐ | ☐ | ☐ |
| Select a location | ☐ | ☐ | ☐ |
| Assess your competition | ☐ | ☐ | ☐ |

| | Completed | In Progress | Yet to Start |
|---|---|---|---|
| Promote your product/service | ☐ | ☐ | ☐ |
| Determine insurance needs | ☐ | ☐ | ☐ |
| Consult with an attorney | ☐ | ☐ | ☐ |
| Consult with an accountant | ☐ | ☐ | ☐ |
| Select a legal structure | ☐ | ☐ | ☐ |
| Estimate needed capital | ☐ | ☐ | ☐ |
| Obtain needed financing | ☐ | ☐ | ☐ |
| Obtain necessary supplies | ☐ | ☐ | ☐ |
| Manage business affairs | ☐ | ☐ | ☐ |
| Plan for future expansion | ☐ | ☐ | ☐ |
| Plan for retirement | ☐ | ☐ | ☐ |

Entrepreneurship is very different from a traditional nine-to-five job. On a job, you get vacations, performance evaluations, and colleagues to socialize with. More importantly, there tends to be a list of job requirements and a supervisor to help you manage your time and meet your goals. On your own, without someone looking over your shoulder, self-management becomes crucial. Consider the questions that follow to help explore critical management issues involved in starting your own small business:

- How big do you want your business to be?

- How much income do you expect to generate?

- How much time do you want to devote to your business?

- How will operating a home-based business affect your lifestyle?

- List the tasks about running a business you dislike (for example, bookkeeping, stuffing envelopes, dealing with customer complaints, and so on).

- What compromises will you make in order to meet your goals?

# Where to Learn More

This book is not intended to offer a crash course in small-business startup (if it were, this would probably be the first chapter rather than the third). It is intended to help you find your career direction, your sense of purpose, and to plan the steps necessary to get there. It might be that self-employment is not a part of your career path; it **may** not even be **something** you are remotely interested in. But if you are interested, and you have an idea of some merit, you owe it to yourself to learn more.

The following resources can help you pursue your dreams of starting your own small business:

- *The Entrepreneur Next Door:* This book, written by Bill Wagner, can help readers explore their strengths and weaknesses as potential entrepreneurs, identify specific types of businesses that suit their personality, and discover the secrets of financial independence.

- *Entrepreneurship For Dummies:* This book, written by Kathleen Allen, can help readers turn their ideas for new business ventures into reality. The book provides practical information and a step-by-step plan for how to become a successful entrepreneur. It provides great advice for everything from putting together a business plan to developing a marketing campaign.

- *Self-Employment: From Dream to Reality:* This workbook, by Linda Gilkerson and Theresia Paauwe, is an excellent resource for beginning entrepreneurs. It is for people who have little or no experience in running their own business, do not have a lot of money to invest, and are trying to decide if self-employment is for them.

- **http://www.guru.com:** On this Web site, entrepreneurs can create a profile that details who they are and what services they offer.

- **http://www.elance.com:** This Web site places entrepreneurs in a virtual workplace to offer their services or business ideas to potential customers.

- **http://www.freeagent.com:** On this Web site, freelance workers or consultants are matched with potential employers based on the skills each entrepreneur has to offer.

---
**NOTE**

The latest statistics suggest that women are 12 times more likely to become self-employed than men. One theory suggests that women have always had to rely more on self-employment because their career patterns have always been more complex than that of men. Regardless of the statistics, nothing says that one gender has a better chance of succeeding as an entrepreneur than the other.

---

Also, know that it is in your best interest to consult with an attorney and an accountant before you make decisions about starting your own business. They can help you with legal and insurance issues, tax planning, and the advantages and disadvantages of different kinds of business structures.

Most importantly, as with any career decision, you should discuss your plans for self-employment with friends and family. Career change, by its very nature, can be risky, and self-employment often magnifies those risks. Communicate your ideas and goals to the people who will be affected by your decisions, and take their advice to heart. After all, you will need their support most of all as you pursue the dream of being your own boss.

# Tying It All Together

More and more people are forgoing the traditional workplace in search of work that they can direct and that provides meaning. Many people find that entrepreneurial pursuits are the only way to find the ideal job. Now might be the perfect time to start your own business. Your current career transition might provide a great opportunity to test the entrepreneurial waters.

Having reflected on the nature of your transition, established your current needs, and assessed your potential for self-employment, you are ready to jump-start your career by focusing on the kind of work that will bring you the most satisfaction. Part II will help you explore career options by assessing your skills, interests, values, and personality. But don't forget what you've learned about yourself so far. Build on it by integrating that self-knowledge into your new discoveries to forge a career path that is right for you.

The worksheet on the following page can help you summarize and reflect on what you've discovered so far.

# Part I Summary: Define Your Purpose

Taken individually, your results on the three assessments in this section can provide insight into a particular aspect of your career path or identity. Taken together, they provide a starting point for further career exploration and development.

Based on the results of the assessments and the information you completed in each chapter, use the following worksheet to summarize what you've discovered about yourself. This information can help you make important career decisions as you work through the rest of the book.

| EXERCISE |
|---|

My career development style (from chapter 1): _____

| **Advantages of that style** | **Disadvantages of that style** |
|---|---|
| _____ | _____ |
| _____ | _____ |
| _____ | _____ |

The *kind* of career path I'd like to take based on my style:

_____

_____

My most pressing career needs (from chapter 2):

_____

_____

Ways my work could help me better fulfill those needs:

_____

_____

Ways other life roles can help me fulfill those needs:

_____

_____

My degree of entrepreneurial readiness (from chapter 3):

_____

Possible ideas I have for starting my own business:

_____

_____

Based on the information above, what will it take for me to feel more satisfied with my job and career?

_____

_____

What possible jobs or activities can I engage in that will match my intended career path, satisfy my most pressing needs, and/or help me fulfill my dream of becoming self-employed?

_____

_____

# PART II: DISCOVER YOUR IDEAL JOB

*"The point of life is not to slave away for years until the age of 65 and then say 'Phew, glad that's over!' Rather, it is to make sure that we do not die with our music still in us."*
—*Lance Secretan, author of* Living the Moment: A Sacred Journey

# CHAPTER 4

# Discover Your Skills and Interests

*"Life is the sum of your choices."*
*—Albert Camus*

Jenny works as an admissions counselor in a small college. She loves her job. She answers questions by phone, helps students gather information about the college, and recruits students from local high schools. As part of her job, Jenny sometimes does intricate math problems in her head. Students who know her well often bring their math homework to her for help. One day, a student told Jenny that she should quit her job as a counselor and become an accountant. She looked horrified. "No way. Not me," she said. "I would hate to be cooped up all day in an office counting. I need to be around people!"

One secret to career satisfaction and success is to find an occupation that matches both your interests and your abilities. Recent studies of young adults making a career change found that nearly half of them changed occupations to find a better fit between their skills and interests.

It seems that the two would correlate and that people who were interested in something would also be good at it, but this isn't always the case, as the example above shows. Achieving career success, then, becomes a balancing act between finding work that you enjoy and work at which you excel.

Discovering where your skills and interests overlap can clue you in to the kinds of occupations that suit you.

# Who Am I and What Am I Doing Here?

If you've ever asked this at work (either question, really), you might have been experiencing a disconnect in your work identity. In other words, who you think you are and what you think you are good at don't gel with the role you fill at work.

Don't be discouraged. Many of us have asked these questions in the face of jobs that didn't satisfy us–that didn't hold our interest or make good use of our abilities. It's that moment where you look around you–at your cubicle or your uniform or the tool in your hand–and say, "This isn't me." After all, who doesn't want a career that fits them so that he or she can look around and say, "Now, this–*this*–is me"?

Unfortunately, the process of matching yourself to that ideal job isn't easy. It often requires a lot of trial and error. Most importantly, it involves knowing who you are and what you can do. That means knowing how your interests, skills, values, and personality traits all contribute to your overall career.

The idea that you could more successfully match yourself to a career by exploring your interests, skills, and other personal traits began with the career guidance movement in the first part of the twentieth century. It was Frank Parsons, a vocational guidance counselor, who called for a better way to help people choose occupations. Parsons's theory, referred to as the "trait-and-factor approach," became the foundation for career counseling programs in the twentieth century.

The theory works under the assumption that all people have a unique pattern of traits that can be objectively measured and compared with the requirements of various occupations. Parsons's process for doing this was really quite simple: He compared an individual's personal characteristics with the characteristics required for successful performance in different jobs. The closer the match between individual traits and job requirements, the more productive and satisfied the person would be in that line of work. For Parsons and, in fact, for many career counselors and coaches today, that process begins by assessing your interests.

## THE "RIGHT" OCCUPATION IS THE WRONG APPROACH

Much of Parsons's work still holds up today. Vocational counselors, job coaches, high school teachers, and college counselors still dole out assessments to students and clients with the hope of helping them make more informed career decisions. However, some of the assumptions behind the trait-factor approach haven't stood time's test. Namely, Parsons believed that there was one "right" occupation for each person and that a single type of person works in each job–ideas that don't hold much water in a world where the average adult changes jobs more often than he or she changes addresses. Don't try to find the "right" job–just try to find the best one for you.

# Taking an Interest in Interests

Interests are constellations of the things you like and dislike. You show your interests through the activities you engage in, what you value, what you like to talk about, and your patterns of behavior. When you were a kid, you were probably asked what you wanted to be when you grew up. In most cases, this question ends up being about interests. An early interest in basketball, ballet, music, or movies can have a dramatic impact on an eight-year-old's long-term career plans.

---

**EXERCISE**

What were you interested in as a child? And what is your answer to that clichéd question?

My interests growing up:

_____

_____

What I wanted to be when I grew up:

_____

---

Your interests have probably changed over the years. Interests we have as children are influenced by our family and social background, our friends and teachers, and the recreational activities we are exposed to. Interests we have as children tend to be unstable, however, and are often not useful in our career planning as adults (although some of us do carry the dreams of our adolescence with us and grow up to be astronauts, fire-fighters, or movie stars).

Our interests evolve. We learn more, experience new things, engage in new relationships, and play a variety of roles. Our needs sometimes dictate our interests, regulating how much time, money, or energy we have to invest in them. No matter how old we are or what stage in life we're at, it's always important to fuel our interests, as they are a constant source of our career and life satisfaction.

**NOTE**

If you already know what your interests are, why bother taking an assessment? The truth is that even people who know what their interests are don't know how to translate those interests into occupations. By clarifying your interests and seeing how they relate to the world of work, you will make better decisions.

---

**EXERCISE**

In the space below, list the interests you currently have. Feel free to list as many as you can think of. Compare them to the interests you had as a child. How much has changed?

_____

_____

_____

---

Research suggests that interests are a major determinant of both college major and occupational choice and that they are the most important considerations in finding a good fit between you and the world of work.

# The Career Interest Inventory

This assessment can help you explore career and job alternatives based on your interests. Read each item, decide how much you would enjoy engaging in that activity, and check the appropriate response using the following scale:

**4 = Very Interested    3 = Somewhat Interested    2 = A Little Interested    1 = Not Interested**

This is not a test. Since there are no right or wrong answers, do not spend too much time thinking about your responses. Be sure to respond to every statement. Do not worry about totaling your scores at this point.

| How interested are you in... | Very Interested | Somewhat Interested | A Little Interested | Not Interested |
|---|---|---|---|---|
| 1. planting and trimming trees | 4 | 3 | 2 | 1 |
| 2. managing and protecting natural resources | 4 | 3 | 2 | 1 |
| 3. caring for sick animals | 4 | 3 | 2 | 1 |
| 4. working on a farm | 4 | 3 | 2 | 1 |
| 5. studying the composition of soil | 4 | 3 | 2 | 1 |
| 6. conducting experiments with plants | 4 | 3 | 2 | 1 |

Section 1 Total: _____

| | Very Interested | Somewhat Interested | A Little Interested | Not Interested |
|---|---|---|---|---|
| **How interested are you in...** | | | | |
| 7. assembling products from wood | 4 | 3 | 2 | 1 |
| 8. operating heavy equipment | 4 | 3 | 2 | 1 |
| 9. working with tools | 4 | 3 | 2 | 1 |
| 10. using drafting instruments to prepare detailed drawings | 4 | 3 | 2 | 1 |
| 11. planning, designing, and directing construction projects | 4 | 3 | 2 | 1 |
| 12. creating safe and functional buildings | 4 | 3 | 2 | 1 |

**Section 2 Total:** _____

| | Very Interested | Somewhat Interested | A Little Interested | Not Interested |
|---|---|---|---|---|
| **How interested are you in...** | | | | |
| 13. researching and writing news stories | 4 | 3 | 2 | 1 |
| 14. singing in a professional choir | 4 | 3 | 2 | 1 |
| 15. preparing public relations information | 4 | 3 | 2 | 1 |
| 16. painting or sketching landscapes or portraits | 4 | 3 | 2 | 1 |
| 17. doing commercial art or design projects | 4 | 3 | 2 | 1 |
| 18. dancing in a variety show or acting in a play | 4 | 3 | 2 | 1 |

**Section 3 Total:** _____

| | Very Interested | Somewhat Interested | A Little Interested | Not Interested |
|---|---|---|---|---|
| **How interested are you in...** | | | | |
| 19. supervising and motivating others | 4 | 3 | 2 | 1 |
| 20. adding columns of numbers | 4 | 3 | 2 | 1 |
| 21. leading and making important decisions for people | 4 | 3 | 2 | 1 |
| 22. computing wages for payroll records | 4 | 3 | 2 | 1 |
| 23. managing a department or an organization | 4 | 3 | 2 | 1 |
| 24. completing tax forms for corporations or individuals | 4 | 3 | 2 | 1 |

**Section 4 Total:** _____

| | Very Interested | Somewhat Interested | A Little Interested | Not Interested |
|---|---|---|---|---|
| **How interested are you in...** | | | | |
| 25. teaching reading, English, or math | 4 | 3 | 2 | 1 |
| 26. watching children at a day care center | 4 | 3 | 2 | 1 |
| 27. managing education programs | 4 | 3 | 2 | 1 |
| 28. working with special-needs students | 4 | 3 | 2 | 1 |
| 29. teaching life skills to adults | 4 | 3 | 2 | |
| 30. tutoring students having trouble in school | 4 | 3 | 2 | 1 |

**Section 5 Total:** _____

| | Very Interested | Somewhat Interested | A Little Interested | Not Interested |
|---|---|---|---|---|
| **How interested are you in...** | | | | |
| 31. analyzing and tracking investments | 4 | 3 | 2 | 1 |
| 32. preparing financial reports | 4 | 3 | 2 | 1 |
| 33. buying and selling stocks and bonds | 4 | 3 | 2 | 1 |

*(continued)*

*(continued)*

| | Very Interested | Somewhat Interested | A Little Interested | Not Interested |
|---|---|---|---|---|
| 34. studying financial trends | 4 | 3 | 2 | 1 |
| 35. selling insurance policies | 4 | 3 | 2 | 1 |
| 36. helping people plan their retirement | 4 | 3 | 2 | 1 |

**Section 6 Total:** _____

**How interested are you in...**

| | Very Interested | Somewhat Interested | A Little Interested | Not Interested |
|---|---|---|---|---|
| 37. examining financial documents for errors | 4 | 3 | 2 | 1 |
| 38. making plans for land use in cities | 4 | 3 | 2 | 1 |
| 39. inspecting tree damage and preventing forest fires | 4 | 3 | 2 | 1 |
| 40. keeping accounting records for a government agency | 4 | 3 | 2 | 1 |
| 41. conducting research for crime prevention agencies | 4 | 3 | 2 | 1 |
| 42. investigating crimes | 4 | 3 | 2 | 1 |

**Section 7 Total:** _____

**How interested are you in...**

| | Very Interested | Somewhat Interested | A Little Interested | Not Interested |
|---|---|---|---|---|
| 43. diagnosing and treating illnesses | 4 | 3 | 2 | 1 |
| 44. helping people overcome physical disabilities | 4 | 3 | 2 | 1 |
| 45. working as an aide in a hospital | 4 | 3 | 2 | 1 |
| 46. working on a rescue squad | 4 | 3 | 2 | 1 |
| 47. helping people maintain healthy teeth | 4 | 3 | 2 | 1 |
| 48. researching diseases and cures | 4 | 3 | 2 | 1 |

**Section 8 Total:** _____

**How interested are you in...**

| | Very Interested | Somewhat Interested | A Little Interested | Not Interested |
|---|---|---|---|---|
| 49. teaching tourists to scuba dive | 4 | 3 | 2 | 1 |
| 50. preparing and/or serving meals | 4 | 3 | 2 | 1 |
| 51. helping people plan trips as a travel guide | 4 | 3 | 2 | 1 |
| 52. cutting and styling hair | 4 | 3 | 2 | 1 |
| 53. leading tourists on a mountain-climbing expedition | 4 | 3 | 2 | 1 |
| 54. managing a hotel or motel | 4 | 3 | 2 | 1 |

**Section 9 Total:** _____

**How interested are you in...**

| | Very Interested | Somewhat Interested | A Little Interested | Not Interested |
|---|---|---|---|---|
| 55. helping students manage stress effectively | 4 | 3 | 2 | 1 |
| 56. working in a mental health clinic | 4 | 3 | 2 | 1 |
| 57. helping people in crises | 4 | 3 | 2 | 1 |
| 58. providing marriage counseling | 4 | 3 | 2 | 1 |
| 59. doing social service work | 4 | 3 | 2 | 1 |
| 60. working with at-risk youth | 4 | 3 | 2 | 1 |

**Section 10 Total:** _____

| | Very Interested | Somewhat Interested | A Little Interested | Not Interested |
|---|---|---|---|---|
| **How interested are you in...** | | | | |
| 61. repairing computers | 4 | 3 | 2 | 1 |
| 62. helping people use technology | 4 | 3 | 2 | 1 |
| 63. managing an organization's computer network | 4 | 3 | 2 | 1 |
| 64. writing computer programs and software | 4 | 3 | 2 | 1 |
| 65. creating or managing Web sites | 4 | 3 | 2 | 1 |
| 66. finding new ways to prevent computer viruses | 4 | 3 | 2 | 1 |

**Section 11 Total:** _____

| | Very Interested | Somewhat Interested | A Little Interested | Not Interested |
|---|---|---|---|---|
| **How interested are you in...** | | | | |
| 67. helping people solve legal problems | 4 | 3 | 2 | 1 |
| 68. using equipment to fight fires | 4 | 3 | 2 | 1 |
| 69. collecting evidence to solve a criminal case | 4 | 3 | 2 | 1 |
| 70. enforcing laws and regulations | 4 | 3 | 2 | 1 |
| 71. preparing and arguing legal cases for trial | 4 | 3 | 2 | 1 |
| 72. protecting people and property from harm | 4 | 3 | 2 | 1 |

**Section 12 Total:** _____

| | Very Interested | Somewhat Interested | A Little Interested | Not Interested |
|---|---|---|---|---|
| **How interested are you in...** | | | | |
| 73. setting up machines according to written standards | 4 | 3 | 2 | 1 |
| 74. producing precision metal and wood products | 4 | 3 | 2 | 1 |
| 75. operating lathes and drill presses | 4 | 3 | 2 | 1 |
| 76. disassembling and repairing machinery | 4 | 3 | 2 | 1 |
| 77. repairing televisions and other electronic devices | 4 | 3 | 2 | 1 |
| 78. inspecting and evaluating the quality of products | 4 | 3 | 2 | 1 |

**Section 13 Total:** _____

| | Very Interested | Somewhat Interested | A Little Interested | Not Interested |
|---|---|---|---|---|
| **How interested are you in...** | | | | |
| 79. selling products over the Internet | 4 | 3 | 2 | 1 |
| 80. planning advertising campaigns | 4 | 3 | 2 | 1 |
| 81. raising funds for an organization | 4 | 3 | 2 | 1 |
| 82. persuading others to buy something | 4 | 3 | 2 | 1 |
| 83. helping people buy and sell homes | 4 | 3 | 2 | 1 |
| 84. explaining and demonstrating how to use products | 4 | 3 | 2 | 1 |

**Section 14 Total:** _____

| | Very Interested | Somewhat Interested | A Little Interested | Not Interested |
|---|---|---|---|---|
| **How interested are you in...** | | | | |
| 85. solving difficult math problems | 4 | 3 | 2 | 1 |
| 86. conducting chemistry experiments | 4 | 3 | 2 | 1 |
| 87. collecting and analyzing rocks | 4 | 3 | 2 | 1 |

*(continued)*

*(continued)*

| | Very Interested | Somewhat Interested | A Little Interested | Not Interested |
|---|---|---|---|---|
| 88. studying the nature of the universe | 4 | 3 | 2 | 1 |
| 89. researching and developing products for a corporation | 4 | 3 | 2 | 1 |
| 90. creating and interpreting maps, graphs, and diagrams | 4 | 3 | 2 | 1 |
| Section 15 Total: _____ | | | | |
| **How interested are you in...** | | | | |
| 91. maintaining automobile engines | 4 | 3 | 2 | 1 |
| 92. driving a truck or taxi cab | 4 | 3 | 2 | 1 |
| 93. driving a bus from city to city | 4 | 3 | 2 | 1 |
| 94. doing auto body repairs | 4 | 3 | 2 | 1 |
| 95. flying airplanes or helicopters | 4 | 3 | 2 | 1 |
| 96. transporting passengers and cargo | 4 | 3 | 2 | 1 |
| Section 16 Total: _____ | | | | |

# Scoring

The Career Interest Inventory is made up of 16 sections representing 16 major career clusters. Those clusters, in turn, represent the majority of available occupations. For each section on the previous pages, add the numbers you circled for each item. Put that total on the line at the end of each section. The higher the total number for each section, the more important it is for you to pursue those types of interests when making career decisions. For each scale, a score from 6—12 is low, a score from 13—18 is average, and a score from 19—24 is high.

Later in this chapter, you will use your results to reveal possible occupations of interest. But first, you need to think about your skills.

# What Are Skills?

Skills are things that you are able to do well, such as playing chess, working on car engines, shooting free throws, or writing speeches. Most people have hundreds or even thousands of skills, many of which they use daily and some they may not even be aware of. Skills are also those capabilities that you bring with you to the workplace. They are activities that you do in order to help employers reach their goals.

## WHERE SKILLS ARE DEVELOPED

Skills are not just learned at work; you can develop them in a variety of roles and settings, including the following:

- **At home:** Some skills are learned in the home, including budgeting and financial planning, planning family vacations, motivating kids to clean their room, negotiating, organizing schedules, chauffeuring, and cooking.

- **In school:** Many skills are developed at school, including writing, critical thinking, creative problem solving, working as part of a team, tutoring others, conducting research, and calculating math problems.

- **In the community:** Skills are learned while engaged in community activities, including organizing neighborhood events, volunteering at a library, serving as president of an organization, being a statistician for athletic events, and organizing religious or spiritual activities.

Because you can gain them from a wide variety of activities and then transfer them from one task to another, skills have become more important in today's world of work. It's important for you not only to discover the various skills that you possess, but also to identify the skills you most enjoy using.

People interested in making a career change need to be keenly aware of how they can apply their skills to a variety of jobs. After all, a corporate executive who suddenly decides to teach high school needs to make good use of his or her negotiation skills when the erasers start flying. Likewise, a stay-at-home mom should consider her time-management skills when thinking about a new career after the nest empties. By assessing your skills, you can better

- Identify your strengths and weaknesses.

- Determine abilities that are important in your work.

- Assess your self-confidence and self-esteem.

- Examine and consider career alternatives.

- Formulate a career objective.

## YOU CAN TAKE THEM WITH YOU

Transferable skills are those skills that are not job specific but cut horizontally across all industries and vertically across all jobs, from entry level to chief executive. Transferable skills are portable skills that people take from one life experience to another. They include such skills as building things, instructing people, analyzing data, leading a group, and managing money. Transferable skills naturally develop from all aspects of life–especially from activities outside work–and then carry over to a job.

Before you jump into the assessment that follows, take some time to think about your best skills. They don't necessarily have to be skills that you used in previous jobs, although it helps if you could use them in some kind of work (writing with your toes or being able to stick your fist in your mouth, while impressive, aren't likely to earn you a paycheck).

---

**EXERCISE**

List what you believe to be your 10 best skills below:

_____    _____

_____    _____

_____    _____

_____    _____

_____    _____

---

# The Career Skills Inventory

The Career Skills Inventory can help you think about and identify the skills you possess that you can transfer to the world of work. You may have acquired these skills from working at various full- or part-time jobs or through leisure activities, volunteer experiences, hobbies, classes, and training experiences.

Please read each statement carefully. Then, using the following scale, circle the number that best describes your degree of skill:

**3 = Very Skilled    2 = Somewhat Skilled    1 = A Little Skilled    0 = Not Skilled or N/A**

This is not a test. Since there are no right or wrong answers, do not spend too much time thinking about your responses. Be sure to respond to every statement. Do not worry about totaling your scores at this point.

| | Very Skilled | Some- what Skilled | A Little Skilled | Not Skilled or N/A |
|---|---|---|---|---|
| **In working with plants and animals, how skilled are you at the following tasks?** | | | | |
| Sitting for pets | 3 | 2 | 1 | 0 |
| Weeding | 3 | 2 | 1 | 0 |
| Grooming pets | 3 | 2 | 1 | 0 |
| Gardening | 3 | 2 | 1 | 0 |
| Tree trimming | 3 | 2 | 1 | 0 |
| Planting | 3 | 2 | 1 | 0 |
| Breeding pets | 3 | 2 | 1 | 0 |
| Landscaping | 3 | 2 | 1 | 0 |

| | Very Skilled | Some- what Skilled | A Little Skilled | Not Skilled or N/A |
|---|---|---|---|---|
| Farming | 3 | 2 | 1 | 0 |
| Training pets | 3 | 2 | 1 | 0 |
| **Section 1 Total: _____** | | | | |
| **In working with designing and maintaining build-ings, how skilled are you at the following tasks?** | | | | |
| Building | 3 | 2 | 1 | 0 |
| Wiring | 3 | 2 | 1 | 0 |
| Remodeling | 3 | 2 | 1 | 0 |
| Repairing | 3 | 2 | 1 | 0 |

| | Very Skilled | Some-what Skilled | A Little Skilled | Not Skilled or N/A |
|---|---|---|---|---|
| Plumbing | 3 | 2 | 1 | 0 |
| Wallpapering | 3 | 2 | 1 | 0 |
| Measuring | 3 | 2 | 1 | 0 |
| Reading blueprints | 3 | 2 | 1 | 0 |
| Drafting | 3 | 2 | 1 | 0 |
| Using power tools | 3 | 2 | 1 | 0 |

**Section 2 Total:** _____

**In expressing your ideas creatively, how skilled are you at the following tasks?**

| | Very Skilled | Some-what Skilled | A Little Skilled | Not Skilled or N/A |
|---|---|---|---|---|
| Singing | 3 | 2 | 1 | 0 |
| Dancing | 3 | 2 | 1 | 0 |
| Photography | 3 | 2 | 1 | 0 |
| Drawing | 3 | 2 | 1 | 0 |
| Writing | 3 | 2 | 1 | 0 |
| Performing | 3 | 2 | 1 | 0 |
| Editing | 3 | 2 | 1 | 0 |
| Designing | 3 | 2 | 1 | 0 |
| Painting | 3 | 2 | 1 | 0 |
| Sculpting | 3 | 2 | 1 | 0 |

**Section 3 Total:** _____

**In making an organization, project, or club run smoothly, how skilled are you at the following tasks?**

| | Very Skilled | Some-what Skilled | A Little Skilled | Not Skilled or N/A |
|---|---|---|---|---|
| Supervising processes | 3 | 2 | 1 | 0 |
| Coordinating events | 3 | 2 | 1 | 0 |
| Planning projects | 3 | 2 | 1 | 0 |
| Budgeting | 3 | 2 | 1 | 0 |
| Directing activities | 3 | 2 | 1 | 0 |
| Delegating authority | 3 | 2 | 1 | 0 |
| Managing resources | 3 | 2 | 1 | 0 |
| Bookkeeping | 3 | 2 | 1 | 0 |
| Filing | 3 | 2 | 1 | 0 |
| Motivating employees | 3 | 2 | 1 | 0 |

**Section 4 Total:** _____

**In helping people learn, how skilled are you at the following tasks?**

| | Very Skilled | Some-what Skilled | A Little Skilled | Not Skilled or N/A |
|---|---|---|---|---|
| Evaluating | 3 | 2 | 1 | 0 |
| Coaching | 3 | 2 | 1 | 0 |
| Teaching | 3 | 2 | 1 | 0 |
| Training | 3 | 2 | 1 | 0 |
| Planning lessons | 3 | 2 | 1 | 0 |
| Encouraging | 3 | 2 | 1 | 0 |
| Counseling | 3 | 2 | 1 | 0 |
| Mentoring | 3 | 2 | 1 | 0 |
| Testing knowledge | 3 | 2 | 1 | 0 |
| Explaining ideas | 3 | 2 | 1 | 0 |

**Section 5 Total:** _____

**In helping people and organizations become financially fit, how skilled are you at the following tasks?**

| | Very Skilled | Some-what Skilled | A Little Skilled | Not Skilled or N/A |
|---|---|---|---|---|
| Accounting | 3 | 2 | 1 | 0 |
| Interviewing | 3 | 2 | 1 | 0 |
| Calculating | 3 | 2 | 1 | 0 |
| Analyzing data | 3 | 2 | 1 | 0 |
| Tracking investments | 3 | 2 | 1 | 0 |
| Managing inventory | 3 | 2 | 1 | 0 |
| Auditing | 3 | 2 | 1 | 0 |
| Financial planning | 3 | 2 | 1 | 0 |
| Selling | 3 | 2 | 1 | 0 |
| Investing | 3 | 2 | 1 | 0 |

**Section 6 Total:** _____

**In helping government agencies meet the needs of the public, how skilled are you at the following tasks?**

| | Very Skilled | Some-what Skilled | A Little Skilled | Not Skilled or N/A |
|---|---|---|---|---|
| Campaigning | 3 | 2 | 1 | 0 |
| Lobbying | 3 | 2 | 1 | 0 |
| Inspecting facilities | 3 | 2 | 1 | 0 |
| Planning projects | 3 | 2 | 1 | 0 |
| Reporting results | 3 | 2 | 1 | 0 |
| Proofreading documents | 3 | 2 | 1 | 0 |
| Compiling statistics | 3 | 2 | 1 | 0 |
| Entering data | 3 | 2 | 1 | 0 |

*(continued)*

*(continued)*

| | Very Skilled | Some- what Skilled | A Little Skilled | Not Skilled or N/A |
|---|---|---|---|---|
| Keeping records | 3 | 2 | 1 | 0 |
| Evaluating progress | 3 | 2 | 1 | 0 |

Section 7 Total: _____

**In helping people be healthy, how skilled are you at the following tasks?**

| | | | | |
|---|---|---|---|---|
| Caring for others | 3 | 2 | 1 | 0 |
| Nursing | 3 | 2 | 1 | 0 |
| Treating injuries | 3 | 2 | 1 | 0 |
| Researching cures | 3 | 2 | 1 | 0 |
| Examining specimens | 3 | 2 | 1 | 0 |
| Diagnosing illnesses | 3 | 2 | 1 | 0 |
| Performing experiments | 3 | 2 | 1 | 0 |
| Healing | 3 | 2 | 1 | 0 |
| Fixing teeth | 3 | 2 | 1 | 0 |
| Dispensing medicines | 3 | 2 | 1 | 0 |

Section 8 Total: _____

**In helping meet other people's needs, how skilled are you at the following tasks?**

| | | | | |
|---|---|---|---|---|
| Cutting/styling hair | 3 | 2 | 1 | 0 |
| Entertaining | 3 | 2 | 1 | 0 |
| Cooking/baking | 3 | 2 | 1 | 0 |
| Serving others | 3 | 2 | 1 | 0 |
| Playing sports | 3 | 2 | 1 | 0 |
| Cleaning | 3 | 2 | 1 | 0 |
| Nurturing | 3 | 2 | 1 | 0 |
| Guiding tours | 3 | 2 | 1 | 0 |
| Planning events | 3 | 2 | 1 | 0 |
| Traveling in foreign countries | 3 | 2 | 1 | 0 |

Section 9 Total: _____

**In helping other people improve their overall well-being, how skilled are you at the following tasks?**

| | | | | |
|---|---|---|---|---|
| Helping others cope | 3 | 2 | 1 | 0 |
| Monitoring client progress | 3 | 2 | 1 | 0 |
| Empathizing | 3 | 2 | 1 | 0 |
| Solving problems | 3 | 2 | 1 | 0 |

| | Very Skilled | Some- what Skilled | A Little Skilled | Not Skilled or N/A |
|---|---|---|---|---|
| Mentoring | 3 | 2 | 1 | 0 |
| Helping the disabled | 3 | 2 | 1 | 0 |
| Camp counseling | 3 | 2 | 1 | 0 |
| Facilitating groups | 3 | 2 | 1 | 0 |
| Listening | 3 | 2 | 1 | 0 |
| Studying behavior | 3 | 2 | 1 | 0 |

Section 10 Total: _____

**In designing, developing, and supporting information systems, how skilled are you at the following tasks?**

| | | | | |
|---|---|---|---|---|
| Programming computers | 3 | 2 | 1 | 0 |
| Creating Web sites | 3 | 2 | 1 | 0 |
| Repairing computers | 3 | 2 | 1 | 0 |
| Analyzing systems | 3 | 2 | 1 | 0 |
| Maintaining networks | 3 | 2 | 1 | 0 |
| Technical writing | 3 | 2 | 1 | 0 |
| Analyzing data | 3 | 2 | 1 | 0 |
| Designing software | 3 | 2 | 1 | 0 |
| Applying software | 3 | 2 | 1 | 0 |
| Securing networks | 3 | 2 | 1 | 0 |

Section 11 Total: _____

**In protecting people and property, how skilled are you at the following tasks?**

| | | | | |
|---|---|---|---|---|
| Researching personal backgrounds | 3 | 2 | 1 | 0 |
| Rehabilitating people | 3 | 2 | 1 | 0 |
| Enforcing regulations | 3 | 2 | 1 | 0 |
| Investigating crimes | 3 | 2 | 1 | 0 |
| Guarding property | 3 | 2 | 1 | 0 |
| Inspecting buildings | 3 | 2 | 1 | 0 |
| Fighting fires | 3 | 2 | 1 | 0 |
| Defending yourself and others | 3 | 2 | 1 | 0 |
| Handling firearms | 3 | 2 | 1 | 0 |
| Arguing a particular viewpoint | 3 | 2 | 1 | 0 |

Section 12 Total: _____

**In using machines to process materials, how skilled are you at the following tasks?**

| | Very Skilled | Some- what Skilled | A Little Skilled | Not Skilled or N/A |
|---|---|---|---|---|
| Repairing broken machines | 3 | 2 | 1 | 0 |
| Assembling products | 3 | 2 | 1 | 0 |
| Installing new components | 3 | 2 | 1 | 0 |
| Maintaining machines | 3 | 2 | 1 | 0 |
| Setting up machines | 3 | 2 | 1 | 0 |
| Drilling | 3 | 2 | 1 | 0 |
| Welding | 3 | 2 | 1 | 0 |
| Grinding | 3 | 2 | 1 | 0 |
| Forging | 3 | 2 | 1 | 0 |
| Operating heavy machinery | 3 | 2 | 1 | 0 |

Section 13 Total: _____

**In persuading others or bringing them to your point of view, how skilled are you at the following tasks?**

| | Very Skilled | Some- what Skilled | A Little Skilled | Not Skilled or N/A |
|---|---|---|---|---|
| Marketing | 3 | 2 | 1 | 0 |
| Making an argument | 3 | 2 | 1 | 0 |
| Promoting products | 3 | 2 | 1 | 0 |
| Selling | 3 | 2 | 1 | 0 |
| Demonstrating products | 3 | 2 | 1 | 0 |
| Raising money | 3 | 2 | 1 | 0 |
| Writing proposals | 3 | 2 | 1 | 0 |
| Publicizing events | 3 | 2 | 1 | 0 |
| Speaking publicly | 3 | 2 | 1 | 0 |
| Communicating ideas | 3 | 2 | 1 | 0 |

Section 14 Total: _____

**In learning more about the natural world, life sciences, and human behavior, how skilled are you at the following tasks?**

| | Very Skilled | Some- what Skilled | A Little Skilled | Not Skilled or N/A |
|---|---|---|---|---|
| Teaching | 3 | 2 | 1 | 0 |
| Inventing | 3 | 2 | 1 | 0 |
| Discovering | 3 | 2 | 1 | 0 |
| Studying unexplained phenomena | 3 | 2 | 1 | 0 |
| Conceptualizing research | 3 | 2 | 1 | 0 |
| Formulating theories | 3 | 2 | 1 | 0 |
| Reviewing data | 3 | 2 | 1 | 0 |
| Conducting experiments | 3 | 2 | 1 | 0 |
| Doing library research | 3 | 2 | 1 | 0 |
| Systematizing data | 3 | 2 | 1 | 0 |

Section 15 Total: _____

**In moving people or materials, how skilled are you at the following tasks?**

| | Very Skilled | Some- what Skilled | A Little Skilled | Not Skilled or N/A |
|---|---|---|---|---|
| Estimating distances | 3 | 2 | 1 | 0 |
| Planning routes | 3 | 2 | 1 | 0 |
| Driving long distances | 3 | 2 | 1 | 0 |
| Operating heavy machinery | 3 | 2 | 1 | 0 |
| Piloting boats | 3 | 2 | 1 | 0 |
| Navigating ships | 3 | 2 | 1 | 0 |
| Operating a train | 3 | 2 | 1 | 0 |
| Unloading packages and materials | 3 | 2 | 1 | 0 |
| Flying aircraft | 3 | 2 | 1 | 0 |
| Delivering goods | 3 | 2 | 1 | 0 |

Section 16 Total: _____

# Scoring

The Career Skills Inventory is made up of 16 sections representing the same 16 major career clusters as the Career Interest Inventory. For each section on the previous pages, add the numbers you circled for each item. Put that total on the line at the end of each section. The higher the total number for each section, the more skills you perceive yourself to have in that particular career cluster. For each scale, a score from 0—10 is low, a score from 11—20 is average, and a score from 21—30 is high.

# Matching Your Interests and Skills to Occupations

You can use your results from the assessments you just completed to narrow down your career possibilities. For each cluster that follows, list your score from the Career Interest Inventory in the blank marked "Interest" and whether it was low, average, or high. Similarly, list your score from the Career Skills Inventory in the blank marked "Skill" and whether it was low, average, or high. Keep in mind that you may have a high interest in a cluster but a low skill level. The opposite can also be true. Of course, just because you don't have the skills related to a particular career doesn't mean you shouldn't pursue it–skills can be learned, after all. You should, however, begin your exploration with career clusters in which you have both a high interest and a high skill level.

1. **Agriculture and Natural Resources:** An interest in working with plants, animals, forests, or mineral resources for agriculture, horticulture, conservation, and other purposes.

   **Interest:** _____   **Skill:** _____

2. **Architecture and Construction:** An interest in designing, assembling, and maintaining buildings and other structures.

   **Interest:** _____   **Skill:** _____

3. **Arts and Communication:** An interest in creatively expressing feelings or ideas, in communicating news or information, or in performing.

   **Interest:** _____   **Skill:** _____

4. **Business and Administration:** An interest in making an organization run smoothly.

   **Interest:** _____   **Skill:** _____

5. **Education and Training:** An interest in helping people learn.

   **Interest:** _____   **Skill:** _____

6. **Finance and Insurance:** An interest in helping businesses and people secure their financial futures.

   **Interest:** _____   **Skill:** _____

7. **Government and Public Administration:** An interest in helping a government agency serve the needs of the public.

   **Interest:** _____   **Skill:** _____

8. **Health Science:** An interest in helping people and animals be healthy.

   **Interest:** _____   **Skill:** _____

9. **Hospitality, Tourism, and Recreation:** An interest in catering to the wishes and needs of others so that they may enjoy a clean environment, good food and drink, comfortable accommodations, and worthwhile recreation.

   **Interest:** _____ **Skill:** _____

10. **Human Service:** An interest in improving people's social, mental, emotional, or spiritual well-being.

    **Interest:** _____ **Skill:** _____

11. **Information Technology:** An interest in designing, developing, managing, and supporting information systems.

    **Interest:** _____ **Skill:** _____

12. **Law and Public Safety:** An interest in upholding people's rights or in protecting people and property.

    **Interest:** _____ **Skill:** _____

13. **Manufacturing:** An interest in turning materials into products or maintaining and repairing products by using machines or hand tools.

    **Interest:** _____ **Skill:** _____

14. **Retail and Wholesale Sales and Service:** An interest in bringing others to a particular point of view through personal persuasion and sales techniques.

    **Interest:** _____ **Skill:** _____

15. **Scientific Research, Engineering, and Mathematics:** An interest in discovering, collecting, and analyzing information about the natural world, life sciences, and human behavior.

    **Interest:** _____ **Skill:** _____

16. **Transportation, Distribution, and Logistics:** An interest in operations that move people or materials.

    **Interest:** _____ **Skill:** _____

Looking back over your results, which career clusters yielded the highest combined scores? Use the following space to list the four career clusters with the highest scores. This provides an excellent clue as to the kind of occupation you will find the most satisfying.

_____         _____

_____         _____

The following lists a sampling of career options for each cluster. Starting with the four you listed above, read through the list of job titles, checking any that sound interesting to you. Do not worry about the education and training required for these jobs. For now, just isolate potential careers that you would consider pursuing.

## AGRICULTURE AND NATURAL RESOURCES

- ☐ Agricultural Engineer
- ☐ Animal Scientist
- ☐ Animal Trainer
- ☐ Conservation Worker
- ☐ Construction Driller
- ☐ Environmental Engineer
- ☐ Farm Manager
- ☐ Farmer
- ☐ Fisher
- ☐ Food Scientist
- ☐ Forester
- ☐ Groundskeeper
- ☐ Nursery and Greenhouse Manager
- ☐ Park Naturalist
- ☐ Pest Control Worker
- ☐ Petroleum Engineer
- ☐ Rancher
- ☐ Soil Conservationist
- ☐ Tree Trimmer
- ☐ Veterinarian
- ☐ Zoologist

## ARCHITECTURE AND CONSTRUCTION

- ☐ Architect
- ☐ Brickmason
- ☐ Building Inspector
- ☐ Bulldozer Operator
- ☐ Carpenter
- ☐ Ceiling Tile Installer
- ☐ Construction Manager
- ☐ Crane Operator
- ☐ Drafter

- ☐ Drywall Installer
- ☐ Electrician
- ☐ Heating and Air Conditioning Mechanic
- ☐ Home Appliance Installer
- ☐ Insulation Worker
- ☐ Painter
- ☐ Paperhanger
- ☐ Pipelayer
- ☐ Plumber
- ☐ Roofer
- ☐ Stonemason
- ☐ Surveyor

## ARTS AND COMMUNICATION

- ☐ Actor
- ☐ Art Director
- ☐ Broadcast News Analyst
- ☐ Cartoonist
- ☐ Choreographer
- ☐ Composer
- ☐ Dancer
- ☐ Editor
- ☐ Fashion Designer
- ☐ Graphic Designer
- ☐ Interior Designer
- ☐ Interpreter or Translator
- ☐ Musician
- ☐ Painter
- ☐ Photographer
- ☐ Public Relations Manager
- ☐ Radio and Television Announcer
- ☐ Reporter
- ☐ Sculptor

☐ Sound Engineering Technician

☐ Writer

## BUSINESS AND ADMINISTRATION

☐ Accountant

☐ Administrative Assistant

☐ Auditor

☐ Brokerage Clerk

☐ Budget Analyst

☐ Chief Executive

☐ File Clerk

☐ Human Resources Manager

☐ Legal Secretary

☐ Management Analyst

☐ Medical Secretary

☐ Meeting and Convention Planner

☐ Office Clerk

☐ Personnel Recruiter

☐ Post Office Clerk

☐ Secretary

☐ Shipping Clerk

☐ Tax Preparer

## EDUCATION AND TRAINING

☐ Adult Education Teacher

☐ Archivist

☐ Curator

☐ Educational Counselor

☐ Elementary School Teacher

☐ Fitness Trainer

☐ Instructional Coordinator

☐ Kindergarten Teacher

☐ Librarian

☐ Library Assistant

☐ Middle School Teacher

☐ Museum Technician

☐ Postsecondary Teacher

☐ Preschool Teacher

☐ Secondary School Teacher

☐ Special Education Teacher

☐ Teacher Assistant

☐ Vocational Education Teacher

## FINANCE AND INSURANCE

☐ Advertising Sales Agent

☐ Appraiser

☐ Assessor

☐ Bank Teller

☐ Bill and Account Collector

☐ Cost Estimator

☐ Credit Checker

☐ Financial Analyst

☐ Financial Manager

☐ Insurance Adjuster

☐ Insurance Underwriter

☐ Loan Counselor

☐ Loan Officer

☐ Market Research Analyst

☐ Personal Financial Advisor

☐ Securities and Commodities Salesperson

☐ Survey Researcher

☐ Treasurer

## GOVERNMENT AND PUBLIC ADMINISTRATION

☐ Agricultural Inspector

☐ Aviation Inspector

☐ City Planning Aide

☐ Court Clerk

- ☐ Court Reporter
- ☐ Environmental Compliance Inspector
- ☐ Equal Opportunity Representative
- ☐ Financial Analyst
- ☐ Fire Inspector
- ☐ Fish and Game Warden
- ☐ Government Property Inspector
- ☐ Immigration and Customs Inspector
- ☐ License Clerk
- ☐ Licensing Examiner
- ☐ Missing Persons Investigator
- ☐ Municipal Clerk
- ☐ Tax Examiner or Collector
- ☐ Urban Planner

## HEALTH SCIENCE

- ☐ Anesthesiologist
- ☐ Athletic Trainer
- ☐ Audiologist
- ☐ Cardiovascular Technologist
- ☐ Chiropractor
- ☐ Coroner
- ☐ Dental Assistant or Hygienist
- ☐ Dentist
- ☐ Diagnostic Medical Sonographer
- ☐ Dietician or Nutritionist
- ☐ Home Health Aide
- ☐ Laboratory Technician
- ☐ Massage Therapist
- ☐ Medical Transcriptionist
- ☐ Nurse
- ☐ Occupational Therapist
- ☐ Optician

- ☐ Pediatrician
- ☐ Pharmacist
- ☐ Psychiatrist
- ☐ Radiologic Technologist
- ☐ Respiratory Therapist
- ☐ Surgeon
- ☐ Veterinarian

## HOSPITALITY, TOURISM, AND RECREATION

- ☐ Amusement Attendant
- ☐ Baker
- ☐ Bartender
- ☐ Butcher
- ☐ Concierge
- ☐ Cook
- ☐ Counter Attendant
- ☐ Flight Attendant
- ☐ Gaming Dealer or Manager
- ☐ Hairdresser
- ☐ Host or Hostess
- ☐ Hotel Desk Clerk
- ☐ Janitor
- ☐ Lodging Manager
- ☐ Maid
- ☐ Recreation Worker
- ☐ Ticket Agent
- ☐ Tour Guide
- ☐ Travel Agent
- ☐ Usher
- ☐ Waiter or Waitress

## HUMAN SERVICE

- ☐ Child Care Worker
- ☐ Clergy

☐ Clinical Psychologist

☐ Counselor

☐ Funeral Attendant

☐ Interviewer

☐ Marriage and Family Therapist

☐ Mental Health Counselor

☐ Nanny

☐ Personal and Home Care Aide

☐ Probation Officer

☐ Rehabilitation Counselor

☐ Residential Advisor

☐ Social and Human Services Assistant

☐ Social Worker

## INFORMATION TECHNOLOGY

☐ Artificial Intelligence/Robotics Programmer

☐ Computer and Information Systems Manager

☐ Computer Facilities Manager

☐ Computer Operator

☐ Computer Programmer

☐ Computer Scientist

☐ Computer Security Specialist

☐ Computer Software Engineer

☐ Computer Systems Analyst

☐ Data Processing Equipment Repairer

☐ Database Administrator

☐ Network Administrator

☐ Office Machine Repairer

☐ Systems Analyst

☐ Web Developer

## LAW AND PUBLIC SAFETY

☐ Arbitrator

☐ Bailiff

☐ Correctional Officer

☐ Criminal Investigator

☐ EMT or Paramedic

☐ Fire Investigator

☐ Firefighter

☐ Highway Patroller

☐ Judge

☐ Law Clerk

☐ Lawyer

☐ Lifeguard

☐ Paralegal

☐ Police Detective

☐ Private Detective

☐ Security Guard

☐ Sheriff or Deputy Sheriff

☐ Title Searcher

## MANUFACTURING

☐ Aircraft Engine Specialist

☐ Appliance Repairer

☐ Automotive Specialty Technician

☐ Bookbinder

☐ Cabinetmaker

☐ Industrial Production Manager

☐ Jeweler

☐ Machinist

☐ Molding and Casting Worker

☐ Powerplant Operator

☐ Printing Machine Operator

☐ Production Laborer

☐ Semiconductor Processor

☐ Slaughterer or Meatpacker

☐ Soldering Machine Operator

☐ Stationary Engineer

☐ Tool and Die Maker

☐ Woodworker

**RETAIL AND WHOLESALE SALES AND SERVICE**

☐ Adjustment Clerk

☐ Advertising Manager

☐ Cashier

☐ Counter and Rental Clerk

☐ Customer Service Representative

☐ Demonstrator

☐ Funeral Director

☐ Marketing Manager

☐ Model

☐ Purchasing Agent

☐ Real Estate Broker

☐ Receptionist and Information Clerk

☐ Retail Salesperson

☐ Sales Manager

☐ Telemarketer

**SCIENTIFIC RESEARCH, ENGINEERING, AND MATHEMATICS**

☐ Actuary

☐ Anthropologist

☐ Archaeologist

☐ Astronomer

☐ Biologist

☐ Chemist

☐ Economist

☐ Engineer

☐ Engineering Technician

☐ Epidemiologist

☐ Geographer

☐ Historian

☐ Materials Scientist

☐ Mechanical Drafter

☐ Physicist

☐ Sociologist

☐ Statistician

☐ Surveying Technician

**TRANSPORTATION, DISTRIBUTION, AND LOGISTICS**

☐ Able Seaman

☐ Airline Pilot or Flight Engineer

☐ Ambulance Driver

☐ Bus Driver

☐ Cargo and Freight Agent

☐ Courier

☐ Driver/Sales Worker

☐ Freight Inspector

☐ Locomotive Engineer

☐ Postal Service Mail Carrier

☐ Public Transportation Inspector

☐ Subway or Streetcar Operator

☐ Taxi Driver or Chauffeur

☐ Traffic Technician

☐ Truck Driver

Of all the occupations you just checked, which seem the most interesting to you? List the 10 occupations you'd most like to explore in more detail in the space below.

---

**EXERCISE**

**Ten Occupations I Would Like to Learn More About**

_____     _____
_____     _____
_____     _____
_____     _____
_____     _____

---

# My Ideal Job

No job is likely to incorporate all your interests or use all your skills. And it doesn't have to. Interests or skills that go unsatisfied through our work are often satisfied through other aspects of our lives, like our leisure activities.

However, your job—and the career it contributes to—will serve as one of the most important, if not the most important, conduit for developing your interests and skills. With that in mind, it helps to know what to look for as you search for the best job to meet your needs. In the space below, write down interests you want to pursue and the skills you'd like to use in your ideal job.

---

**EXERCISE**

| Interests | Skills |
| --- | --- |
| _____ | _____ |
| _____ | _____ |
| _____ | _____ |
| _____ | _____ |

---

# Tying It All Together

Now that you have determined what your career interests and skills are, you are well on your way to choosing an occupation that will lead you to career success. Remember that interests are those things that you are most passionate about and feel called to take part in. However, they are just one part of the career equation. Hopefully, your skills will correlate with your interests. If not, you should consider finding ways to get those skills, either through additional education, on-the-job training, or other means.

But even skills and interests don't give you the entire picture. Your work preferences are made up of a complex interaction of many other factors. The next chapter will help you to learn more about what you value in your career.

# CHAPTER 5

# Identify Your Values

*"A person who simply settles for whatever comes his/her way, rather than pursuing his/her own goals, is probably not living a life based upon his/her own freely chosen values. He/she usually ends up by feeling that life is not very meaningful or satisfying."*
*—Sidney Simon, Leland Howe, and Howard Kirschenbaum in* Values Clarification

Kali is a college student considering work as a counselor. She enjoys volunteering at a retirement community on the weekends. She says she wants to "make the world a better place." She really doesn't care how much money she makes (she is majoring in social work, after all). She just wants to nurture others and make a difference in their lives. She values generosity and community service and isn't really interested in climbing any corporation's ladder.

Sharon is the chief executive officer of a large company. She makes gobs of money and enjoys the "finer" things in life: her 3,500-square-foot condo, her new Mercedes, and her summer vacations in Europe. She loves being recognized as one of the most successful female CEOs in the country. She enjoys setting goals for herself and then working hard to achieve them, knowing that she helps make her company, her stockholders, and herself very wealthy.

James is an anthropology professor at a medium-size university. He loves learning about new things and teaching what he knows to others. He has written several books on the topic of ancient civilizations, and you can often find him in the library, poring over old books and maps. He makes enough money to live comfortably, but he prefers the rewards that come from teaching and research: the summers off, the interactions with students, and the chance to intellectually challenge himself every day.

# Work and Values

People choose to enter certain occupations because they value the rewards they receive from the work they do. Whether it's helping people, making money, or continuing to learn, the values that motivate people to work vary considerably, and no single value appeals to everyone equally. Although you share common values with people from all over the world, you have a value system that is unique to you.

Values are beliefs and behaviors that are important to you—that provide you with a sense of usefulness, meaning, and worth. For example, my friend Rick values financial security over all else. He wants to retire early and have enough money to live comfortably for the next 30 or 40 years. This value affects his life in many ways: He doesn't take expensive vacations or eat out often, and he puts the maximum amount in his retirement account each year. He has stayed at the same job most of his working life and has tried his best to move up the corporate ladder. Rick's situation is unique in that he has one major value that dominates his career. Most of us have two or three or more.

## WHERE DO VALUES COME FROM?

Our values are developed in the early years of life through a combination of environment and experiences. Most experts on the topic of values suggest that you develop them from interactions with your parents, siblings, teachers, friends, coaches, neighbors, and all parts of the community in which you live.

Some values are learned through reading or even from movies and television. (Think of the many generations who have learned to share by watching *Sesame Street*.) It is through explanations, modeling, rewards, punishments, and rules that these influential forces in your life provide the basis for your value system.

Unlike the people in the preceding examples, not all of us have such clear-cut value systems. In today's chaotic world of work, we are confronted with more choices than previous generations. We are besieged by messages telling us what to value through advertising, as well as from parents, friends, teachers, and coworkers. Do we value low prices or high living? Do we value the safety and prestige of a monstrous four-wheel-drive or the environmental friendliness of a hybrid economy car? Do we value the security that comes with saving for retirement or the desire to live for the moment and spend every last cent while we're young? Our values are there to guide us—to help answer those questions, determine our actions, and define our goals.

**NOTE**

While many see values as simply principles of right and wrong, such a definition is limiting. Although morality plays a significant role in your value system, your values also include your beliefs about what is meaningful to you. They help you prioritize what is most important.

Your values also dictate the amount of motivation you have toward your work and other activities. Your personal values, to a large extent, help determine job satisfaction. Thus, understanding your values—and how they relate to the world of work—is an important step in pursuing the type of career and lifestyle you desire.

# The Work Values Scale

This assessment can help you identify and explore your dominant values and how these values affect your career development. It contains 60 activity statements directly related to potential values in your life and career.

Read each statement, and then circle the number to the right that best describes how important the activity is to you according to the following scale:

**4 = Very Important     3 = Important     2 = Somewhat Important     1 = Unimportant**

This is not a test. Since there are no right or wrong answers, do not spend too much time on each item. Be sure to respond to every statement.

| How important is it for you to... | Very Important | Important | Somewhat Important | Unimportant |
|---|---|---|---|---|
| Read and/or write poetry | 4 | 3 | 2 | 1 |
| Create beautiful things | 4 | 3 | 2 | 1 |
| Brainstorm new ideas | 4 | 3 | 2 | 1 |
| Imagine and design how things will work | 4 | 3 | 2 | 1 |
| Draw or paint | 4 | 3 | 2 | 1 |
| Develop new skills working with your hands | 4 | 3 | 2 | 1 |
| Make music | 4 | 3 | 2 | 1 |
| Invent new products | 4 | 3 | 2 | 1 |
| Attend theater performances | 4 | 3 | 2 | 1 |
| Visit museums or art galleries | 4 | 3 | 2 | 1 |

Section 1 Total: _____

| How important is it for you to... | Very Important | Important | Somewhat Important | Unimportant |
|---|---|---|---|---|
| Analyze numerical data | 4 | 3 | 2 | 1 |
| Use computers to solve problems | 4 | 3 | 2 | 1 |
| Use statistics in your daily life | 4 | 3 | 2 | 1 |
| Understand complex mathematical problems | 4 | 3 | 2 | 1 |
| Use deductive reasoning | 4 | 3 | 2 | 1 |
| Be an expert at learning and remembering numbers | 4 | 3 | 2 | 1 |
| Calculate and compute numbers easily | 4 | 3 | 2 | 1 |
| Manage your money effectively | 4 | 3 | 2 | 1 |
| Be able to follow complex instructions | 4 | 3 | 2 | 1 |
| Be detail oriented | 4 | 3 | 2 | 1 |

Section 2 Total: _____

*(continued)*

*(continued)*

| How important is it for you to... | Very Important | Important | Somewhat Important | Unimportant |
|---|---|---|---|---|
| Do volunteer work | 4 | 3 | 2 | 1 |
| Be understanding of others' problems | 4 | 3 | 2 | 1 |
| Give to worthwhile charities | 4 | 3 | 2 | 1 |
| Share your time and money with others | 4 | 3 | 2 | 1 |
| Do social service work | 4 | 3 | 2 | 1 |
| Counsel other people | 4 | 3 | 2 | 1 |
| Teach | 4 | 3 | 2 | 1 |
| Ensure the safety and well-being of the public | 4 | 3 | 2 | 1 |
| Be a positive role model | 4 | 3 | 2 | 1 |
| Help people in need | 4 | 3 | 2 | 1 |

**Section 3 Total:** _____

| How important is it for you to... | Very Important | Important | Somewhat Important | Unimportant |
|---|---|---|---|---|
| Make important decisions | 4 | 3 | 2 | 1 |
| Be a leader | 4 | 3 | 2 | 1 |
| Be the boss rather than an employee | 4 | 3 | 2 | 1 |
| Manage group projects | 4 | 3 | 2 | 1 |
| Plan long-term goals | 4 | 3 | 2 | 1 |
| Be considered a business expert | 4 | 3 | 2 | 1 |
| Be financially successful | 4 | 3 | 2 | 1 |
| Manage others' work | 4 | 3 | 2 | 1 |
| Be admired by other business leaders | 4 | 3 | 2 | 1 |
| Be in a position of authority | 4 | 3 | 2 | 1 |

**Section 4 Total:** _____

| How important is it for you to... | Very Important | Important | Somewhat Important | Unimportant |
|---|---|---|---|---|
| Display good hand-eye coordination | 4 | 3 | 2 | 1 |
| Be outdoors | 4 | 3 | 2 | 1 |
| Be engaged in sporting events | 4 | 3 | 2 | 1 |
| Have good motor skills | 4 | 3 | 2 | 1 |
| Work at mechanical activities | 4 | 3 | 2 | 1 |
| Make things with your hands | 4 | 3 | 2 | 1 |
| Grow plants | 4 | 3 | 2 | 1 |
| Use hand tools like hammers and screwdrivers | 4 | 3 | 2 | 1 |
| Operate large machines and equipment | 4 | 3 | 2 | 1 |
| Be able to repair things in your home | 4 | 3 | 2 | 1 |

**Section 5 Total:** _____

| How important is it for you to... | Very Important | Important | Somewhat Important | Unimportant |
|---|---|---|---|---|
| Learn all you can about science | 4 | 3 | 2 | 1 |
| Construct or interpret maps and graphs | 4 | 3 | 2 | 1 |
| Study and test hypotheses | 4 | 3 | 2 | 1 |
| Collect biological data | 4 | 3 | 2 | 1 |
| Understand all you can about plants or animals | 4 | 3 | 2 | 1 |
| Conduct scientific experiments | 4 | 3 | 2 | 1 |
| Read about scientific or medical discoveries | 4 | 3 | 2 | 1 |
| Read about technical developments | 4 | 3 | 2 | 1 |
| Work with the knowledge and processes of the sciences | 4 | 3 | 2 | 1 |
| Solve complex problems | 4 | 3 | 2 | 1 |
| Section 6 Total: _____ | | | | |

## Scoring

Add the numbers you have circled for each section. Put that total in the space marked "Total" at the end of each section. Then, transfer your totals for each section to the lines below. The higher the number for each section, the more important those work values are to you in making satisfying career and life choices.

Section 1: Artistic _____     Section 2: Logical _____     Section 3: Social _____

Section 4: Authoritative _____     Section 5: Physical _____     Section 6: Scientific _____

# Understanding Your Values

Research by Hunter Lewis helped create the assessment that you just completed. Lewis was a prominent researcher who spent his life studying human behavior–specifically, what motivated people to do the things they do. Lewis was president of the American School of Classical Studies in Athens, Greece, where he developed a system for categorizing values that are important in a person's life and career. His book *A Question of Values: Six Ways We Make the Personal Choices That Shape Our Lives* broke all values into six overarching categories or systems:

- **Artistic:** People with this type of value system express a dominant interest in beauty, harmony, imagination, and the pursuit of art and creative expression. They are interested in turning intuition into artistic creations. (Lewis called this the Intuition Value System.)

- **Logical:** People with this type of value system express a dominant interest in using deductive logic, dialectics, and advanced mathematical tools to solve problems and make decisions. (Lewis called this the Logical Value System.)

- **Social:** People with this type of value system express a dominant interest in altruism and philanthropy, helping other people, and nurturing and caring for others. (Lewis called this the Emotional Value System.)

- **Authoritative:** People with this type of value system express a dominant interest in having power and influence, as they value competition and leadership as ways to achieve power. (Lewis called this the Authoritative Value System.)

- **Physical:** People with this type of value system express a dominant interest in the use of their physical prowess, hand-eye coordination, and agility. (Lewis called this the Sensory Experience Value System.)

- **Scientific:** People with this type of value system express a dominant interest in the exploration of the nature of the world or of human beings. They are interested in collecting data and doing scientific research. (Lewis called this the Science Value System.)

Lewis felt that these six systems not only describe how we think about things in general but also describe how our values develop and how we use them in our lives and careers. Most of us will privilege one or two of these values above others, although we will have several of them at more moderate levels. We may even value one or two of these values negatively. (Someone with predominately social values may also privilege scientific values but may eschew authoritative values.) By understanding your work values, you can begin to make career decisions based on those things you care about most deeply.

Of course, few–if any–career options will fully incorporate all your values. What is most important is that you make career decisions that match the values you feel most passionate about. Thus, values you scored high in (scores of 31 or more) represent those values you should try to incorporate into your work. Those you scored low in (20 or fewer) represent values that your work and career need not necessarily encompass. This isn't to suggest that those values aren't important to you–only that they aren't as high a priority.

**EXERCISE**

Think about the values that you identified by taking this assessment to answer the following questions:

What surprised you the most about your results?

_____

_____

What did not surprise you at all?

_____

_____

What did you learn about yourself and your values?

_____

_____

# Tying Values to Occupations

People who carefully consider what they most value in life and in a career are often the ones who land jobs and develop careers that provide satisfying rewards. Therefore, it is important to develop a framework for your values and how they relate to occupations in the real world.

By completing the assessment in this chapter, you have taken the first step in understanding and applying your value system. The next step is for you to examine how your personal value system influences your preferences for certain occupations and work environments.

For each of the following sections, read the descriptions and then consider how your own values match with what is described and with the occupations that follow. Be sure to check any that interest you.

You should begin by focusing on the scale on which you scored highest. This is likely the value system that drives and will continue to drive your career decisions. If you scored high on two or more scales, you should take the time to read each description and then select occupations of interest.

> **NOTE**
>
> Remember that this assessment, like the others in this part of the book, is not a crystal ball. Remember to keep your options open. You will have an opportunity to methodically narrow them down in Part III.

## *Artistic Values*

People with high artistic values enjoy working in jobs where they can create things of beauty. They prefer to engage in imaginative activities that can be done alone. They value work where they can invent and design new products, communicate news or information, or perform for the public. People scoring high on this scale usually appreciate music and the arts.

Place a check mark in front of those occupations that interest you:

☐ Actor

☐ Advertising Agent

☐ Architect

☐ Barber

☐ Broadcast Technician

☐ Cartoonist

☐ Choreographer

☐ Commercial Artist

☐ Cosmetologist

☐ Creative Writer

☐ Curator

☐ Dancer

☐ Desktop Publisher

☐ Director

☐ Editor

☐ Fashion Designer

☐ Fine Arts Instructor

☐ Florist

☐ Graphic Designer

☐ Jewelry Maker

☐ Makeup Artist

☐ Music Teacher

☐ Musician

☐ Painter

☐ Photographer

☐ Poet

☐ Public Relations Manager

☐ Reporter

☐ Sculptor

☐ Singer

☐ Technical Writer

☐ Web Designer

## *Logical Values*

People with high logical values are most interested in solving problems with deductive reasoning. They value working with numbers and having clearly defined procedures. They enjoy calculating, examining, and interpreting data and financial records.

Place a check mark in front of those occupations that interest you:

☐ Accountant

☐ Actuary

☐ Air Traffic Controller

☐ Architect

☐ Attorney

☐ Auditing Clerk

☐ Bank Examiner

☐ Cartographer

☐ Computer Analyst

☐ Computer Programmer

☐ Distribution Manager

☐ Diversity Manager

☐ Economist

☐ Engineer

☐ Financial Examiner

☐ Financial Planner

☐ Information Technologist

☐ International Marketer

☐ Literary Agent

☐ Mathematician

☐ Nuclear Power Technician

☐ Office Manager

☐ Physicist

☐ Pilot

☐ Real Estate Agent

☐ Salesperson

☐ School Principal

☐ Securities Investor

☐ Statistician

# Social Values

Not surprisingly, individuals with high social values like to work with and help other people. They find satisfaction in making a difference in people's lives. This can come in a variety of forms, from teaching and counseling to providing medical care. They generally enjoy work that allows them to provide services to other people rather than products.

Place a check mark in front of those occupations that interest you:

| | |
|---|---|
| ☐ Art Therapist | ☐ Nurse |
| ☐ Caseworker | ☐ Pharmacist |
| ☐ Child Care Worker | ☐ Physician |
| ☐ College Administrator | ☐ Police Officer |
| ☐ Correctional Treatment Specialist | ☐ Probation Officer |
| ☐ Counselor | ☐ Psychologist |
| ☐ Criminologist | ☐ Rehabilitation Specialist |
| ☐ Funeral Attendant | ☐ School Guidance Counselor |
| ☐ Home Health Aide | ☐ Social Worker |
| ☐ Human Resource Manager | ☐ Special Education Teacher |
| ☐ Interviewer | ☐ Substance Abuse Counselor |
| ☐ Librarian | ☐ Teacher |
| ☐ Marriage and Family Therapist | ☐ Veterinarian |
| ☐ Mental Health Worker | ☐ Vocational Guidance Counselor |
| ☐ Missionary | ☐ Welfare Eligibility Worker |

# Authoritative Values

Individuals with high authoritative values are primarily interested in managing people or running organizations. People scoring high on this scale may enjoy working in positions of leadership, ensuring that people work efficiently or follow the rules. They value guiding others, solving problems, and making decisions.

Place a check mark in front of those occupations that interest you:

| | |
|---|---|
| ☐ Arbitrator | ☐ Chief Financial Officer |
| ☐ Assessor | ☐ Cost Estimator |
| ☐ Attorney | ☐ Diplomat |
| ☐ Bank Loan Officer | ☐ Engineer |
| ☐ Buyer | ☐ Financial Manager |
| ☐ Chief Executive Officer | ☐ Fire Inspector |

□ Funeral Director      □ Pilot

□ Highway Patrol Officer      □ Police Officer

□ Homeland Security Officer      □ Political Campaign Manager

□ Hospital Administrator      □ Psychiatrist

□ Human Resource Manager      □ Public Policy Analyst

□ Intelligence Officer      □ Purchasing Agent

□ International Business Representative      □ Real Estate Manager

□ Judge      □ Sales Manager

□ Magistrate      □ Surgeon

□ Military Officer      □ Warden

## *Physical Values*

Individuals with high physical values are primarily interested in working and playing outdoors. They enjoy tinkering with machines and using their hands. People scoring high on this scale value being physically active.

Place a check mark in front of those occupations that interest you:

□ Aerobic Instructor      □ Fish and Game Warden

□ Agriculture Inspector      □ Fitness Trainer

□ Athletic Coach      □ Immigration Inspector

□ Automobile Mechanic      □ Law Enforcement Officer

□ Avionic Technician      □ Machinist

□ Bus Driver      □ Motor Vehicle Inspector

□ Commercial Truck Diver      □ Occupational Health Specialist

□ Concierge      □ Parks and Recreation Director

□ Construction Worker      □ Pipe Fitter

□ Correctional Officer      □ Professional Athlete

□ Electrician      □ Security Guard

□ Embalmer      □ Tool and Die Maker

□ Fire Inspector      □ Travel Guide

## *Scientific Values*

Individuals with high scientific values want to understand how things work. They value using scientific processes to discover, collect, and analyze information. They may enjoy doing research, using computers, and performing experiments.

Place a check mark in front of those occupations that interest you:

☐ Anthropologist  ☐ Meteorologist

☐ Archaeologist  ☐ Nurse

☐ Astronomer  ☐ Occupational Therapist

☐ Athletic Trainer  ☐ Optician

☐ Biologist  ☐ Optometrist

☐ Chemist  ☐ Pharmacist

☐ Chiropractor  ☐ Physical Therapist

☐ Dentist  ☐ Physician

☐ Dietitian  ☐ Physician Assistant

☐ Forensic Scientist  ☐ Radiological Technician

☐ Geologist  ☐ Veterinarian

☐ Medical Technologist

# Prioritizing Your Values

Now it is time to start narrowing your occupational choices based on your values. In the space below, list your two most important values, starting with the one you scored the highest in. Then, use the second column to list the possible occupations you might be interested in that relate to that value.

| EXERCISE | |
|---|---|
| **Value** | **Occupations of Interest** |
| _____ | _____ |
| _____ | _____ |

Now go through the lists of occupations you just made to identify the six that seem most interesting to you.

---

**EXERCISE**

### Six Occupations I Would Like to Learn More About

_____    _____

_____    _____

_____    _____

---

In a perfect world, you would do work that matches all your values—almost as if your personal philosophy on life and the company motto were one and the same. Unfortunately, no such job exists, and if it did exist, you could have trouble finding it. The reality is that your career satisfaction and success depend on you carefully assessing your situation and your job prospects (including your current job) and making a firm decision about those values that your work absolutely must include, those that you'd like it to include, and those that you can do without. Still, it doesn't hurt to set high goals, as long as you remain open to all possibilities.

---

**EXERCISE**

On the lines below, write down those work values that you most want your job and career to reflect:

_____

_____

_____

_____

---

**— NOTE —**

Remember that your career is a combination of your work and leisure. Your values manifest themselves in both, so as with interests and skills, it is possible (even likely) that you can compensate for work that doesn't satisfy all your values through your other life roles. However, you should avoid work that goes against your most important values.

# Tying It All Together

If you are like most people, exploring your values is probably not something you do regularly. The truth is that assessing values is critical in career exploration. Because the most common reason for career dissatisfaction is a lack of congruence between personal values and the values in the work environment, exploring your value system is important. People who lack this insight generally find themselves struggling to manage a career and leading a life without meaning and commitment. The next chapter will help you discover the role your personality can play in your career choices. Then, you put together your interests, skills, values, and personality to identify career paths that fit you best.

# CHAPTER 6

# Explore Your Personality

*"A preference is an inborn tendency to be, act, or think in a certain way. While we do change and grow, and may seem to be different at various times in our lives, our basic personality style remains the same."*
—*Renee Baron,* What Type Am I?

Jan is a practical person who likes to repair automobiles and prefers any job where he doesn't have to behind a desk all day. He enjoys working with his hands and likes to spend his weekends hiking or fishing.

Karen is an inquisitive person who enjoys solving problems that require a lot of research. She likes being intellectually challenged and enjoys debating ideas and beliefs with other people.

Tyrone is a creative and temperamental person who prefers to express himself in innovative and artistic ways. He works from his home as a graphic artist and spends his free time writing and sketching.

Kathy is a compassionate person who enjoys helping others. She likes to go home from work knowing she has made a difference in someone else's life.

Rosie is an energetic and ambitious person who makes a good living as a sales manager. A natural-born leader, she loves being in charge and pushing her staff to meet their quotas.

Shane is a neat and organized person who people can count on to take care of details. He loves working in an office, making sure coworkers get what they need when they need it.

Do any of these people sound like you or people you know? These examples (albeit oversimplified) illustrate some of the different personality types in the workplace. Personality can best be defined as the ways we differ from one another and how these differences affect our individual behavior. Because we live in a society full of other people with whom we must cooperate and compete to get what we want in life, it is critical for us to understand as much about our personality characteristics (and those of others) as possible.

# What's Your Type?

Your personality is a consistent style of behaviors and emotional reactions that are present from infancy onward, developing as a result of a combination of heredity and environmental experiences. Whether you realize it or not, your personality critically impacts your career development. One key to success is to find a career that complements your personality rather than conflicts with it.

Psychologists and psychiatrists believe that human beings share personality characteristics, which we can then use to classify people. They also believe that such a classification can predict how a person with a given personality will behave in a given situation. Such an approach suggests that you can best describe personality by grouping people with similar characteristics into distinct categories called *personality types.*

---

## POINTS TO REMEMBER

Remember these points about personality types as you progress through this chapter:

- You will probably not change your basic personality type, but you can change behaviors associated with your basic type.

- All types have unique sets of strengths and weaknesses.

- All the information you read about your type may not apply to you all the time.

- People with similar personality types tend to be motivated in the same ways, view the world in similar manners, and engage in similar occupations and leisure activities.

- Sociological factors such as where you were born and raised, your family life, cultural values passed down to you from your parents, and your educational attainment can influence the intensity of your personality type.

- No single type is better than any other type.

---

Your personality type developed primarily during your childhood. By the time you reached your teen years, your personality began to crystallize and become a part of who you are. It is very unlikely that your personality type has shifted much since, as our basic personalities rarely change substantially in adulthood.

Your personality affects your career development in a variety of ways. Namely, it has an impact on

- How you approach making career decisions

- How you interact with coworkers and supervisors

- How well you like the work you are doing

- How you define your strengths and weaknesses

- How you recognize and value diversity in others

- How you solve problems and resolve conflicts

Knowing more about your personality type can help you explain why certain patterns also keep repeating in your career.

The more your personality relates to the work you do, the more likely you are to enjoy your work and feel fulfilled by it. The career assessment that follows can help you identify your personality type, interpret the information you learn about yourself, and then apply it to your career planning.

# The Career Personality Inventory

Many experts think that personality plays as important a role as interests and skills in determining the kinds of jobs people gravitate toward. The logic is simple: The greater the match between your occupation and your personality, the greater life and career satisfaction you will have. Your career personality determines such things as whether you enjoy working indoors or outdoors, with people or with information, or making money or making art (although those two don't have to be exclusive). The assessment that follows can help you identify your career personality and the core career and life themes associated with it.

The Career Personality Inventory contains a series of words that describe various personality traits that you may or may not have. Read each word listed to decide whether the word describes you. If it does describe you, circle the word in the column. If it does not describe you, do not circle the word–simply move to the next word.

> **NOTE**
>
> As you explore possibilities, it is important not to rule any occupation out simply because it requires more education and training than you currently have. We are all lifelong learners, and the need for an apprenticeship, a certification, or even a higher degree should not stand in the way of a satisfying career.

Take your time responding, but be sure to respond to every word listed. This is not a test, so there are no right or wrong answers.

**I consider myself to be** (circle all that apply)

| | | |
|---|---|---|
| Athletic | Honest | Persistent |
| Conforming | Humble | Physical |
| Frank | Mechanical | Practical |
| Genuine | Modest | Self-reliant |
| Handy | Natural | Shy |
| Hardheaded | Outdoorsy | Stable |

**R Total:** _____

**I consider myself to be** (circle all that apply)

| | | |
|---|---|---|
| Analytical | Intellectual | Precise |
| Cautious | Introverted | Rational |
| Complex | Logical | Reserved |
| Critical | Methodical | Scholarly |
| Curious | Modest | Scientific |
| Independent | Pessimistic | Self-controlled |

**I Total:** _____

**I consider myself to be** (circle all that apply)

| | | |
|---|---|---|
| Artsy | Idealistic | Intuitive |
| Complicated | Imaginative | Nonconforming |
| Creative | Impulsive | Open |
| Daydreamy | Independent | Original |
| Emotional | Individualistic | Uncontrolled |
| Expressive | Innovative | Unstructured |

**A Total:** _____

**I consider myself to be** (circle all that apply)

| | | |
|---|---|---|
| Altruistic | Generous | People-oriented |
| Cheerful | Helpful | Responsible |
| Compassionate | Humanistic | Sociable |
| Convincing | Idealistic | Tactful |
| Cooperative | Kind | Understanding |
| Emotional | Patient | Warm |

**S Total:** _____

**I consider myself to be (circle all that apply)**

| | | |
|---|---|---|
| Acquisitive | Bold | Impulsive |
| Adventurous | Charismatic | Optimistic |
| Aggressive | Domineering | Persuasive |
| Ambitious | Energetic | Popular |
| Assertive | Extroverted | Self-confident |
| Attention-getting | Goal-driven | Sociable |

**E Total:** _____

**I consider myself to be (circle all that apply)**

| | | |
|---|---|---|
| Careful | Inhibited | Reserved |
| Conforming | Obedient | Scheduled |
| Conscientious | Orderly | Self-controlled |
| Dependable | Persistent | Structured |
| Detail-oriented | Practical | Thrifty |
| Efficient | Precise | Unimaginative |

**C Total:** _____

# Scoring

Count the total number of items you circled for each section. Put that total on the line marked "Total" at the bottom of each section and then transfer your totals to the spaces below:

**R (Realistic)** _____     **S (Social)** _____

**I (Investigative)** _____     **E (Enterprising)** _____

**A (Artistic)** _____     **C (Conventional)** _____

Generally, the higher your score, the more characteristics you share with others of that personality type. Scores from 13 and above are considered high, while those 5 and below would be considered low.

Identify the scale on which you scored the highest. This is your primary personality type. In the descriptions that follow, you should explore all the occupations listed for that scale. This is especially true if you have one score much higher than the rest. However, if you had high scores on two or more scales, you should explore occupations listed under each type. Bear in mind that the occupations listed under each scale represent only a sample of the jobs that might interest you.

Remember that no assessment can tell you who you should be or what job you should do. They can't choose your career path; they can only help you to better define it. Knowing more about your personality can narrow down the number of jobs you might be interested in pursuing. At the same time, it might reveal possible career directions you hadn't thought about before.

---

### How Others See Me

Charles Cooley, a famous sociologist, said that our personality develops based on the way that others see us; he called this theory "The Looking-Glass Self."

Before you interpret your scores on the assessment, it might be fun to retake it. But this time, you should circle descriptors based on the way that you think others would describe you. This exercise might provide you with important information about your personality. Use a different color pen or pencil as you work through the assessment a second time. Then, answer the questions that follow.

How were your scores on the two versions of the assessment similar?

_____

_____

_____

How were your scores on the two versions of the assessment different?

_____

_____

_____

What does this say about your personality?

_____

_____

_____

---

The following sections will describe the six types and provide a list of occupations that relate to each type for you to explore.

# Holland's Personality Theory

Vocational psychologist John Holland created one of the most enduring theories of career development. Holland suggested that your personality style reflects your preferences for interests and activities and that individuals search for work environments that allow them to express their personalities.

For decades, career counselors have used Holland's personality model to match people with congruent occupations. When your personality type matches the duties required for an occupation, you will find greater career satisfaction. For example, an Investigative person would likely find career satisfaction as a biologist, geologist, or food scientist. On the other hand, an Artistic person might feel dissatisfied with a job that is primarily conventional in nature (such as a bank teller or accountant). Research shows that people who enter occupations that are not compatible with their personality type tend to feel dissatisfied with and highly unstable in their jobs.

---

### ONE SIZE DOESN'T FIT ALL

Holland believed that people would function best in a work environment that matched their personality. But it isn't as simple as finding an Artistic job to go with your Artistic personality. For starters, everyone has a combination of different personality orientations, with one orientation being dominant. None of us are purely Realistic or purely Social. Then, there is the fact that very few jobs cater to only one personality type. Work environments are complex and always changing, requiring workers to deal with a variety of tasks and environments. The goal is simply to discover a career that matches well with your personality (just as it should match with your values, interests, and skills), even if it's not a perfect fit.

---

According to Holland, all people have some combination of the following personality types. Each of the following descriptions represents "pure" types. You will probably see some parts of each description fitting you in different roles you play. Keep this in mind as you read each description and explore occupations of interest.

# *Realistic*

People scoring high on the Realistic scale prefer working with their hands and using tools to build or repair things. They enjoy working with machines rather than with people or behind a desk. They tend to lack an interest in social activities and would much rather be outdoors than indoors.

Realistic personalities are cultivators; they have an urge to make things grow and prosper. Their primary interest is in practical, earthy matters, and they tend to have a no-nonsense approach to life.

Realistic personalities are not always interested in the prestige or financial rewards that come with accomplishments–they simply enjoy getting things done. They also have no interest in being innovative or trying to understand complex ideas. Rather, they enjoy things that are easy to experience and that they can feel, taste, hear, and smell.

Realistic personalities seek stability and security in their career paths. They are reliable, stubborn, autonomous, and true to their word.

**Sample Occupations**

☐ Airline Pilot

☐ Anthropologist

☐ Architectural Drafter

☐ Athletic Trainer

☐ Audiovisual Technician

☐ Automotive Mechanic

☐ Boat Builder

☐ Bricklayer

☐ Carpenter

☐ Cartographer

☐ Construction Worker

☐ Cook

☐ Correctional Officer

☐ Drywall Installer

☐ Electrical Technician

☐ Electrician

☐ Engineer

☐ Firefighter

☐ Geologist

☐ Plumber

☐ Police Officer

☐ Production Supervisor

☐ Prosthetist

☐ Radiologic Technician

☐ Recreation Manager

☐ Roofer

☐ Safety Inspector

☐ Sheet Metal Worker

☐ Truck Driver

☐ Waste Management Worker

# *Investigative*

People scoring high on the Investigative scale enjoy working with ideas and concepts in the fields of mathematics, physical sciences, biological sciences, and social sciences. They are bright and curious and tend to be lifelong students. They are driven by the desire to learn new things and solve life's mysteries. They are often perceived as being scholarly, analytic, critical, curious, introspective, and methodical.

Investigative personalities prefer careers where they can explore ideas, test hypotheses, and develop new theories based on what they've learned. They enjoy debating their ideas with others, but they also spend a lot of time alone gathering information. You often find them working in research laboratories, hospitals, or college classrooms.

Investigative personalities are most comfortable thinking rather than feeling or acting. They are always evaluating, processing, and synthesizing information. They do not become bogged down in details, but they always keep the big picture in mind. For the Investigative personality, understanding life is just as much fun as living it.

## Sample Occupations

- ☐ Actuary
- ☐ Aircraft Mechanic
- ☐ Anesthesiologist
- ☐ Biologist
- ☐ Botanist
- ☐ Chemical Engineer
- ☐ Chemist
- ☐ Chief Information Officer
- ☐ Chiropractor
- ☐ Civil Engineer
- ☐ Computer Programmer
- ☐ Coroner
- ☐ Dentist
- ☐ Economist
- ☐ Electrical Engineer
- ☐ Engineering Technician
- ☐ Financial Analyst
- ☐ Fire Investigator

- ☐ Information Systems Supervisor
- ☐ Market-Research Analyst
- ☐ Mathematician
- ☐ Medical Lab Technician
- ☐ Nurse
- ☐ Optometrist
- ☐ Pharmacist
- ☐ Physician
- ☐ Physicist
- ☐ Psychologist
- ☐ Radiologist
- ☐ Research Analyst
- ☐ Sociologist
- ☐ Statistician
- ☐ Surgeon
- ☐ Veterinarian
- ☐ Veterinary Assistant
- ☐ Zoologist

# Artistic

People scoring high on the Artistic scale seek opportunities for creative self-expression through writing, singing, dancing, art, and theater. They avoid highly structured situations and totally involve themselves in their creative endeavors.

Artistic personalities tend to see life from a holistic perspective that allows them to always be looking at the big picture. This allows them to create novel applications to existing services, products, and projects. They are continually looking for new interests and often have difficulty completing projects, making them long on vision but a little short on action.

Artistic personalities strive to make the world a better place through their creative endeavors. They have a very highly developed aesthetic sense and are often asked to bring new perspectives to traditional problems. They tend to be shy and introverted and thus are sometimes uncomfortable in a more traditional business setting. They find typical night-to-five jobs too restrictive, and they do not like taking orders from other people. Therefore, they tend work alone, toiling tirelessly to see their creations come to fruition.

**Sample Occupations**

- ☐ Actor
- ☐ Announcer
- ☐ Architect
- ☐ Art Director
- ☐ Art Teacher
- ☐ Barber
- ☐ Cartoonist
- ☐ Choreographer
- ☐ Columnist
- ☐ Commentator
- ☐ Commercial Artist
- ☐ Composer
- ☐ Curator
- ☐ Dancer
- ☐ Desktop Publisher
- ☐ Drama Teacher
- ☐ Editor
- ☐ English Teacher
- ☐ Engraver
- ☐ Fashion Designer
- ☐ Film Editor
- ☐ Floral Designer
- ☐ Furniture Designer
- ☐ Graphic Designer
- ☐ Illustrator
- ☐ Interior Designer
- ☐ Jeweler
- ☐ Journalist
- ☐ Librarian
- ☐ Makeup Artist
- ☐ Musical Instrument Repairer
- ☐ Musician
- ☐ Painter
- ☐ Photographer
- ☐ Poet
- ☐ Producer
- ☐ Reporter
- ☐ Screenwriter
- ☐ Sculptor
- ☐ Set Designer
- ☐ Singer
- ☐ Talent Director
- ☐ Translator
- ☐ Tree Trimmer
- ☐ Writer

# *Social*

People who score high on the Social scale have a strong concern for the welfare of others. They like giving their time and resources to teach, support, counsel, cure, and otherwise serve other people. Their mission in life tends to be to remain selfless and give more than they take. As such, they are very compassionate and nurturing.

Social personalities seek to help and work in their community, whether through spiritual service, counseling, teaching, or medicine. They tend to value the spiritual and/or emotional rewards they receive from their work more than the material rewards. Their service gives them a sense of identity and worth. They can sometimes become so driven to help others that it becomes their personal crusade.

Social personalities tend to be very critical and highly vocal about the inhumanities they see in the world. Other people often view them as being idealistic. Because of their unwavering belief in their convictions, they make excellent teachers and leaders. They are very thoughtful and emotional but are equally capable of taking quick and decisive action for the benefit of others.

**Sample Occupations**

- ☐ Adult Literacy Teacher
- ☐ Ambulance Driver
- ☐ Animal Trainer
- ☐ Caseworker
- ☐ Child Care Worker
- ☐ Clergy Member
- ☐ Community Service Manager
- ☐ Correctional Treatment Specialist
- ☐ Counselor
- ☐ Dental Assistant
- ☐ Education Administrator
- ☐ Emergency Medical Technician
- ☐ English Teacher
- ☐ Fitness Trainer
- ☐ Human Services Assistant
- ☐ Librarian
- ☐ Loan Officer
- ☐ Marriage Counselor
- ☐ Medical Assistant
- ☐ Mental Health Worker
- ☐ Music Therapist
- ☐ Nurse
- ☐ Occupational Therapist
- ☐ Parole Officer
- ☐ Police Officer
- ☐ Preschool Teacher
- ☐ Principal
- ☐ Psychologist
- ☐ Radiation Therapist
- ☐ Recreational Therapist
- ☐ Rehabilitation Counselor
- ☐ Social Worker
- ☐ Speech-Language Pathologist
- ☐ Teacher
- ☐ Teacher Aide
- ☐ Travel Guide
- ☐ University Professor
- ☐ Urban Planner
- ☐ Vocational Training Instructor

# *Enterprising*

People who score high on the Enterprising scale prefer activities where they can lead, control, or persuade others to reach a personal or organizational goal. They tend to value the rewards that come with power, status, and a higher-than-average income. They strive to be the best at what they do *and* the first to do it. They are confident, determined, and have natural leadership abilities, although in many cases they just prefer to get things done themselves. They are also highly charismatic, which makes them good at selling their ideas, their products, and themselves.

Enterprising personalities prefer to be in charge. They make decisions quickly and decisively, whether others like it or not. They also tend to understand and appreciate the power of money and strive to attain it, control it, and put it to good use. As such, they often run businesses or start new ones, or invest money for themselves or for others.

Enterprising personalities are usually eager to initiate new projects and take on new challenges. Their confidence and determination make "all things possible" and allow them to succeed in the fast-paced world of business. They tend to focus on positive opportunities rather than negative consequences. Perhaps more than any other personality, they are the most driven to pursue the standard American definition of success: climbing the ladder (or building one of their own) to achieve wealth, prestige, and happiness.

**Sample Occupations**

- ☐ Advertising Sales Agent
- ☐ Appraiser
- ☐ Attorney
- ☐ Buyer
- ☐ Chief Executive
- ☐ Claims Adjuster
- ☐ Communications Consultant
- ☐ Construction Manager
- ☐ Customer Service Representative
- ☐ Demonstrator
- ☐ Economist
- ☐ Education Administrator
- ☐ Financial Analyst
- ☐ Financial Manager
- ☐ Funeral Director
- ☐ Gaming Dealer
- ☐ General Manager
- ☐ Human Resources Manager
- ☐ Insurance Adjuster
- ☐ Insurance Agent
- ☐ Judge
- ☐ Leasing Agent
- ☐ Legislator
- ☐ Loan Officer
- ☐ Management Analyst
- ☐ Meeting and Convention Planner
- ☐ Operations Manager
- ☐ Pharmaceutical Dealer
- ☐ Public Relations Manager
- ☐ Purchasing Agent
- ☐ Real Estate Manager
- ☐ Real Estate Sales Agent

☐ Retail Salesperson        ☐ Sales Manager

☐ Sales Engineer            ☐ Sales Representative

## *Conventional*

People who score high on the Conventional scale tend to be neat, organized, and always under control. They can concentrate on the task at hand and are excellent with details. They are orderly to the point of sometimes being inflexible, and they prefer to follow strict guidelines when doing their work.

Conventional personalities prefer working with data and information rather than with people or ideas. They have extraordinary clerical and numerical skills and are often counted on for their dependability and reliability. They are often found in office environments–crunching numbers, keeping records, and processing data. Practical and hardworking, they enjoy solving problems, provided there is a set procedure to follow. They make excellent day-to-day managers, although they prefer to run and organize things from behind the scenes.

Conventional personalities truly value success in the organizations they work for and will do everything in their power to ensure that success. They are conscientious, stable, thorough, conservative, and enjoy having things run according to plan.

### Sample Occupations

☐ Accountant                    ☐ Freight Inspector

☐ Accounting Assistant          ☐ Human Resources Assistant

☐ Air Traffic Controller        ☐ Insurance Clerk

☐ Auditor                       ☐ Legal Secretary

☐ Bank Teller                   ☐ Library Assistant

☐ Bill and Account Collector    ☐ Media Coordinator

☐ Budget Analyst                ☐ Medical Record Technician

☐ Cartographer                  ☐ Medical Secretary

☐ Cashier                       ☐ Office Clerk

☐ Computer Operator             ☐ Payroll Clerk

☐ Cost Estimator                ☐ Personnel Clerk

☐ Court Clerk                   ☐ Pharmacy Technician

☐ Electronics Assembler         ☐ Post Office Clerk

☐ Employment Clerk              ☐ Proofreader

☐ Financial Counselor           ☐ Reservation and Transportation Ticket Agent

☐ Secretary         ☐ Title Examiner

☐ Shipping Clerk       ☐ Travel Clerk

☐ Tax Preparer        ☐ Utility Clerk

# Finding a Good Fit

Starting with the personality type for which you scored highest, pick the occupations that interest you the most and then list them below. Do the same for your second- and third-highest scores.

---

**EXERCISE**

My highest-scoring personality type: _____

Occupations that interest me:

_____

_____

My second-highest scoring personality type: _____

Occupations that interest me:

_____

_____

My third-highest scoring personality type: _____

Occupations that interest me:

_____

_____

---

Now go through the lists of occupations you just made and circle the six that seem the most interesting to you.

---

**EXERCISE**

**Six Occupations I Would Like to Learn More About**

_____      _____

_____      _____

_____      _____

# Tying It All Together

To find your ideal job, you need direct correspondence between your personality type and the characteristics of that job. If you enjoy a highly structured and methodical work environment, for instance, then you probably won't find much satisfaction as a kindergarten teacher. You should instead consider fields such as accounting, engineering, or math.

It is important to understand that all types are found in all occupations. However, in order to be successful and find career satisfaction, you need a job that comes naturally to you. You now have another important piece in the career decision-making puzzle. Combining this with what you've already learned about your interests, skills, and values gives you a comprehensive assessment of your preferred work environment and should produce a few highly compatible career options.

The worksheet on the following page can help you summarize and reflect on what you've discovered in this part of the book. You will use this information as you begin to plan your career in Part III.

# Part II Summary: Discover Your Ideal Job

In the chapters of this section, you identified career options that match your interests, skills, values, and personality. All these contribute to your career identity and provide insight into the kind of work you are best suited for.

Based on the results of the assessments and the information you completed in each chapter, use the following worksheet to summarize what you've learned about yourself. You can then use this information to verify your current career direction or identify a new one. Regardless, by pulling together your results from all three chapters, you should have a much clearer sense of where to go next.

---

**EXERCISE**

My most important interests and skills (from chapter 4):

_____

_____

Ten occupations that appeal to my interests and skills:

_____    _____

_____    _____

_____    _____

_____    _____

_____    _____

My preferred work values (from chapter 5):

_____

_____

Six occupations that appeal to my values:

_____    _____

_____    _____

_____    _____

My most dominant personality type (from chapter 6):

_____

Six occupations that appeal to my personality:

_____     _____

_____     _____

_____     _____

Look at all the jobs you have listed. What occupations, if any, did you list more than once?

_____     _____

_____     _____

Based on all the information above, list the 10 to 12 occupations you are most interested in pursuing next in your career:

_____     _____

_____     _____

_____     _____

_____     _____

_____     _____

_____     _____

# PART III: DEVELOP A CAREER PLAN

*"A goal without a plan is just a wish."*
*–Antoine de Saint-Exupery*

# CHAPTER 7

# Make a Decision

*"You are now at a crossroads. This is your opportunity to make the most important decision you will ever make. Forget the past.... Who are you now? Who have you decided to become? Make this decision consciously. Make it carefully. Make it powerfully."*
*—Anthony Robbins*

Once you are aware of your needs, values, interests, and skills, it becomes easier to choose a path that's right for you. Once you know your options, you are ready to make a decision.

You cannot casually make decisions about your career. The process of change will be stressful for you and people close to you. Your career decisions will affect how much money you make, how happy you are at work, how much self-esteem you feel, how committed you are to your job, and how well you meet your long-term goals.

When facing a career transition, many people simply take the first opportunity that comes along. But those who successfully manage their careers use proven decision-making strategies. They develop career alternatives, collect information, and methodically select the option that best suits their personal characteristics.

The main goal of this book is to help you make informed career decisions by learning more about yourself and what you have to offer. The main goal of this chapter, however, is to focus specifically on the decision-making process itself—to show you how to make a conscious and powerful decision by identifying and removing some of the common barriers to that process.

# The Nature of Career Decisions

Our careers are constellations of decisions and their consequences. Should I go into the military? If I go to college, what will I major in? Do I want to be a teacher or a doctor? Should I take on the family business or start one of my own? Should I go back and get my master's degree? Should I take the job as supervisor in my department? Is it really time to retire? You will encounter many such decisions over the course of your career, with varying degrees of risk and reward.

You have probably made many decisions to get where you are now. Some likely worked out well; others maybe didn't work at all. Decisions such as which courses to take in high school, whether to become involved in community activities, whether to go to college or straight into the workforce, what type of training to find, and even whether to work overtime can all have an impact on your career. The truth is, you will constantly have to make career decisions, and each decision will have some impact on your future.

---

## What Has Worked and What Hasn't?

Part of understanding where you're going is understanding where you've been. In the spaces below, write down one or two career decisions you've made in the past, whether they worked out, and if not, why not. When it comes to careers, much of our learning comes from revisiting our mistakes.

Decision:

_____

_____

Consequences:

_____

_____

If it didn't work out, why not?

_____

_____

Decision:

_____

_____

Consequences:

_____

_____

If it didn't work out, why not?

_____

_____

Career decisions such as whether to leave a current job, return to college full time, or start a new business are difficult for several reasons:

- **Most career decisions involve risk:** Your life and the lives of your family will change based on your career decisions. Suppose that you decide to quit your job to start your own business. You could risk losing a steady paycheck, retirement and health benefits, and family or leisure time. While these changes aren't assured, they are likely, and they are sacrifices that you need to consider.

- **Most career decisions are uncertain:** If you always knew that doing A would lead to B, career decisions would be easy. However, A has a nagging tendency to jaunt off to C, D, or E instead (or Z, if things really go wonky). If you spend money to return to college to finish a bachelor's degree, you assume that you will make more money when you graduate. This assumption is true most of the time. However, there are waiters and waitresses with bachelor's degrees ready to tell you otherwise.

- **Outside influences affect career decisions:** Sometimes, life will interfere and keep you from making effective career decisions. For example, trailing spouses (a spouse who follows his or her significant other from company to company and city to city as the S.O. moves up the career ladder) must often take jobs based on availability. Therefore, many trailing spouses end up taking jobs that pay less or that do not fit their interests, values, and personality.

- **Family issues often conflict with making career decisions:** Other times, you will have to take the best interest of your family into consideration when making career decisions. An example would be a parent who does not take an "ideal" job in another city because it would uproot children from their schools and friends. Often, career decisions require balancing what is best for you with what is best for all other parties involved.

> **NOTE**
>
> Although you can't deny the impact of past decisions to shape where you presently stand in your career, it is important to focus on the decision you need to make *now*. Learn from past mistakes, but don't let them keep you from taking calculated risks with potentially rich rewards.

The key to making successful career decisions is to reduce the uncertainty, risk, and fear that come with them, and the best way to do that is to use a rational decision-making strategy. The assessment that follows–and the strategies it leads to–will help ensure that you make conscious and careful decisions.

# The Career Decision-Making Scale

The Career Decision-Making Scale contains 40 statements related to how you make decisions in your life and your career. Read each statement to decide whether it describes you. If the statement does describe you, circle the number in the column marked "True." If the statement does not describe you, circle the number in the column marked "False."

Take your time responding, and be sure to respond to every statement. Remember, this is not a test; there are no right or wrong answers.

| In making career decisions... | True | False |
|---|:---:|:---:|
| (A) I let others decide for me | 1 | 2 |
| (B) I consider how my decision will affect others | 2 | 1 |
| (C) I carefully evaluate each option available to me | 2 | 1 |
| (D) I just do what feels right rather than rely on logic | 1 | 2 |
| (E) I am often afraid of the consequences of my decisions | 1 | 2 |
| (A) I am sometimes not sure decisions are worth making | 1 | 2 |
| (B) I do not worry about researching my options | 1 | 2 |
| (C) I am very creative in thinking about possibilities | 2 | 1 |
| (D) I usually take the first alternative available to me | 1 | 2 |
| (E) I am not an effective risk-taker | 1 | 2 |
| (A) I prefer to wait and let things work out by themselves | 1 | 2 |
| (B) I have trouble knowing where to go to gather information about my options | 1 | 2 |
| (C) I take a lot of time to think about all alternatives | 2 | 1 |
| (D) I balance my intuitive, "gut" feelings with careful analysis | 2 | 1 |
| (E) I take action after I make a decision | 2 | 1 |
| (A) I am too afraid I will make the "wrong" decision | 1 | 2 |
| (B) I am good at synthesizing information about myself | 2 | 1 |
| (C) I consider all types of career options, no matter how silly they sound | 2 | 1 |
| (D) I lack the confidence necessary to make decisions | 1 | 2 |
| (E) I do not like to accept the consequences for decisions | 1 | 2 |
| (A) I have a specific procedure I follow in making decisions | 2 | 1 |
| (B) I take my interests and skills into account | 2 | 1 |
| (C) I consider the possible consequences and risks of alternatives | 2 | 1 |
| (D) I am willing to compromise | 2 | 1 |
| (E) I worry that acting on my decision will be too much work | 1 | 2 |

|  | True | False |
|---|---|---|
| (A) I often leave decisions to fate | 1 | 2 |
| (B) I ask others I trust for help in making decisions | 2 | 1 |
| (C) I rarely weigh the "pros" and "cons" | 1 | 2 |
| (D) I let others decide for me | 1 | 2 |
| (E) I create a timeline for taking action | 2 | 1 |
| (A) I procrastinate | 1 | 2 |
| (B) I often feel bogged down with useless information | 1 | 2 |
| (C) I take time to eliminate the least acceptable alternatives | 2 | 1 |
| (D) I am often unable to make up my mind | 1 | 2 |
| (E) I make a commitment to my decision | 2 | 1 |
| (A) I trust my decision-making skills | 2 | 1 |
| (B) I know what my career values are | 2 | 1 |
| (C) I think about possible outcomes of my alternatives | 2 | 1 |
| (D) I have trouble synthesizing information to make a decision | 1 | 2 |
| (E) I draw up a specific plan for acting on my decision | 2 | 1 |
| (A) I have trouble committing to the decision-making process | 1 | 2 |
| (B) I am honest with myself | 2 | 1 |
| (C) I rank all the possibilities based on the information available | 2 | 1 |
| (D) I know I need to make a decision, but I just cannot do it | 1 | 2 |
| (E) I take time to reevaluate decisions I make | 2 | 1 |
| (A) I develop a timeline for making the decision | 2 | 1 |
| (B) I look for patterns in the information I gather | 2 | 1 |
| (C) I rationally weigh all the costs and benefits for each outcome | 2 | 1 |
| (D) I make decisions based on my needs | 2 | 1 |
| (E) I set goals for implementing my decisions | 2 | 1 |

# *Scoring*

This assessment can enrich your understanding of how you make career decisions by breaking the process into five steps. Total the numbers you circled for all the statements marked **(A)**, **(B)**, **(C)**, **(D)**, or **(E)**. You will have a score from 10 to 20 for each letter. Put that number in the corresponding space below for each step in the career decision-making process:

**(A) Defining and Committing to the Decision** _____

**(B) Gathering Information About Self and Situation** _____

**(C) Generating and Analyzing Alternatives** _____

**(D) Selecting the Best Alternative** _____

**(E) Implementing Your Decision** _____

Scores from 10—13 are low and indicate that you may need help with this aspect of the decision-making process. On the other hand, scores from 18—20 are high and indicate that this step of the process shouldn't pose much problem for you.

You should pay particular attention to those steps with the lowest scores. The descriptions that follow can help you increase your understanding of the career decision-making process. Read the information to complete the exercises and help ensure that your next career decision is the best one for you.

While the exercises for each step will most benefit those who scored in the low or average ranges on that corresponding step, any job seeker is bound to discover some useful strategies, regardless of his or her score.

# One Step at a Time

No one makes major career decisions blindly. No one flips a coin to decide his or her next career move (at least I hope not), and "eeny meeny miny mo" is not taught in high schools as an effective career-planning strategy. However, studies show that surprisingly few people undergoing a career transition have a methodical, step-by-step approach to choosing their path.

Thankfully, many different career decision-making systems have been developed over the years. All these theories recommend a logical, practical approach to developing a list of possibilities and then choosing the best among them. The model that follows includes five steps that take you from defining your decision to taking action:

1. **Define the decision you need to make and then commit to it:** What is the decision you are struggling with? For most of us, it is deciding which of the many career options available to us will meet our needs and lead to fulfilling our long-term goals. This could include what kind of job to look for, what degree to pursue, or what business to start.

2. **Gather information about yourself and your situation:** Gather information about your personal characteristics–your interests, skills, values, and personality–and pull together this information. Then, gather information about occupations and educational opportunities that interest you. Combined, this information will help you to make better career decisions.

3. **Generate and analyze your alternatives:** Develop a list of possible occupations or opportunities based on how your personal characteristics match with people happily employed in those occupations.

4. **Select the best alternative:** Draw on your personal information to think about what it would be like to work in each possible occupation. At this stage, you begin to value certain careers with the highest potential for providing you with success and satisfaction.

Once you have weighed all the evidence, you are ready to select the occupation that best matches the qualities you bring to the workplace. If you've done the first three steps thoroughly, this step should be easy (or easier, at least).

5. **Implement your decision:** Put your career decision into action by searching for a new job, returning to school, or starting your own business. If it sounds "easier said than done," that's because it is. But don't worry; later chapters in this book will help you with this step.

Now for some good news: You've already completed the first two steps of this process. In Part I of this book, you explored your current occupational situation, your needs in the world of work, and your potential for self-employment. In Part II, you learned a lot about yourself and identified possible occupations and career paths that match your values, interests, skills, and personality. Using that list of possibilities, you are ready to take the next steps in the process.

# Step 1: Define the Decision You Need to Make and Then Commit to It

From the information you learned about yourself in Part I (chapters 1—3), what is the career decision or decisions you need to make? Some examples might include the following:

- Is there a better job out there for me?

- Is there a different line of work out there that would better fulfill my needs?

- Should I try to change my current job so that it better meets my needs?

- Should I go back to college?

- Should I try to start my own business?

---

**EXERCISE**

In the space below, list the career decision(s) you are facing:

_____

_____

What possible barriers stand in your way to making your decision(s)?

_____

_____

_____

_____

---

*(continued)*

*(continued)*

What can you do to overcome those barriers and commit to making and implementing your career decision(s)?

_____

_____

_____

_____

# Step 2: Gather Information About Yourself and Your Situation

Another important step in making an effective career decision is to learn as much as you can about yourself. You have done a lot of the work already.

## EXERCISE

Go back to the summary for Part II (page 106) and list up to 12 career choices you have chosen to consider. Don't forget to also include any self-employment or educational options here.

_____

_____

_____

_____

_____

_____

Now look at all the occupations you have listed. What themes do you see (all the jobs are helping others, most of the jobs are business-oriented, etc.)?

## EXERCISE

Write your themes below, as they will be useful to you later:

_____

_____

_____

---

**GETTING READY**

Most career development experts agree that good decision making can take place only when you are ready to make a decision. Although that sounds like common sense, it might surprise you how often people make career decisions without preparing themselves mentally for the process. To achieve a state of readiness, you must

- Overcome any desire to procrastinate.

- Overcome any fear of taking risks.

- Overcome any fear of failure.

- Overcome any desire for perfection.

Such fears and desires can act as attitudinal blocks–barriers to the decision-making process. Such mental barriers have developed due to beliefs or ideas that you have accumulated over time since childhood and continue to affect your thinking today. The more attitudinal blocks you possess, the less likely you are to make good career decisions.

---

# Step 3: Generate and Analyze Your Alternatives

Your next step is to research the careers under consideration. Although this will take a lot of time and effort, it is key to helping you determine whether the occupations you listed earlier best fit your career needs. For example, discovering that a job that you've listed pays only $20,000 a year could weigh heavily into your decision (or not, depending on your lifestyle and your affinity for peanut butter and jelly sandwiches). Likewise, learning that an occupation is on the decline and that fewer and fewer jobs might exist in this field in the future may be a red flag to you if you need long-term career stability.

Some of the most popular means of gathering occupational information are discussed in the following sections.

## Reading

You can learn a lot about occupations by reading books and career pamphlets. These resources provide information that you can use to determine whether an occupation fits your personal characteristics. Most job descriptions will include a list of job duties, working conditions, average earnings, the training and education required, and the outlook for that particular occupation. You can compare all this data to the information you gathered about yourself in the first two parts of this book to find a job that screams "Come and get me!"

Use the following sources to gather information about specific occupations of interest to you. Page 122 includes an exploration form to help you record what you learn.

**NOTE**

When researching the possibilities, the goal is to gather as much information as possible. However, it is important to focus on the needs you identified earlier in this book. Have a good understanding of your priorities before you start your research; this will give you some specific things to look for.

- *Occupational Outlook Handbook (OOH):* The *OOH*, developed by the U.S. Department of Labor, presents occupations by career families. For each occupation, the *OOH* provides information about job duties, working conditions, level and places of employment, education and training requirements, job employment outlook, advancement possibilities, earnings, and related occupations. You can find it in most libraries or online at www.bls.gov/oco.

> **NOTE**
>
> Remember the occupational themes you identified earlier? You can use them in your career research. Most career reference sources group occupations into *fields* or *clusters.* If you find a theme in your self-analysis that matches one of those clusters (an "affinity for jobs that help people" matching "service jobs," for example), then that's a clue that some of the other jobs included in that cluster might interest you.

- **Occupational Information Network (O*NET):** O*NET is a computerized database of occupational information. It provides information on nearly 1,000 occupations, including job descriptions, work activities, earnings, education requirements, and correlations with other career resources. It is available at libraries or online at http://online.onetcenter.org/.

- *New Guide for Occupational Exploration (GOE):* This book allows you to explore all major O*NET jobs based on your interests. It also corresponds directly to the 16 career clusters used in chapter 4. Thus, you can use your knowledge of your interests and skills to search directly for even more jobs that would be a good fit.

## Job Shadowing

You can learn a lot about jobs by watching people do the work you are interested in. You should pay particular attention to the types of skills the workers use, the way their work environment is organized, and how much interaction occurs with others. When job shadowing, you should ask questions of the person you are shadowing, but you should also stay out of the way.

## Informational Interviewing

Informational interviewing is a way to gain real-world information and advice on a career of interest to you. Informational interviews help you to develop contacts, gain knowledge about occupations of interest, and learn more about the world of work in general. It involves identifying people who do work that you might like doing and asking them questions related to their current job. Informational interviews

- Help you develop greater social skills that will help you when you actually begin to interview for jobs.

- Allow you to build confidence in your ability to discuss your career interests.

- Might lead to other informational interviews and possibly jobs.

- Help you to refine your knowledge of career fields of interest.

- Help you meet people in career fields similar to the ones you are interested in.

Remember that the purpose of informational interviews is not to look for a job, but to gather information to confirm information about the career field and build contacts that may help you in the future. Questions you should ask in an informational interview include the following:

- How did you prepare for your career?

- What are the most important qualifications (skills, education, personality, etc.) needed to succeed in this field?

- How did you get your job?

- What is a typical workweek like?

- What do you like best (or least) about the work you do?

- What are the salary ranges for positions in this field?

## Talking with People

You can also gain valuable occupational information by talking informally with people in various occupations of interest. Remember, anyone you talk to may also be a source of potential job leads down the road.

## Summing Up

The worksheet that follows can help you summarize the most crucial information about any occupations or career paths that interest you. Feel free to make as many copies as necessary; this will make it easier to compare the possibilities later in the career decision-making process.

# Occupational Information Form

Use this form to learn more about the occupations that interest you. You may read job descriptions in books or online or talk with people working in the occupation, with a career counselor, or with friends and family members.

Occupation: _____

Duties and responsibilities: _____

_____

_____

Nature of the work: _____

_____

_____

How is the work performed? _____

_____

_____

Where is the work done? _____

Do you primarily work with people, data, ideas, or things? _____

_____

What are the working hours? _____

What is the average salary? _____

What is the potential for advancement? _____

What is the long-term outlook for the occupation? _____

What education and training are required? _____

Things you think you would like most about the job: _____

_____

_____

Things you think you would like least about the job: _____

_____

_____

Other important information: _____

_____

_____

_____

# Step 4: Select the Best Alternative

Based on your research, you can now develop a list of occupations that interest you most. After having examined your own personal characteristics and gathered information about occupations, you can also effectively select the best alternative.

Use the Occupational Fit Matrix that follows to identify the occupations that best match your personal characteristics. In the first column, list the occupations you identified earlier. Then, in the columns titled Interests, Skills, Personality, and Values, place a check mark if the occupation matches that characteristic. Finally, in the last column, write down the needs (from chapter 2) you think that occupation could fulfill.

> **NOTE**
>
> There are spaces for 14 possibilities, but if you have more, be sure to list them. Also, keep in mind that the list you create here will likely be different from the one you created at the end of Part II. Over the course of your research, you likely eliminated some options and discovered new ones.

## Occupational Fit Matrix

| Occupation | Interests | Skills | Personality | Values | Needs |
|------------|-----------|--------|-------------|--------|-------|
| | | | | | |
| | | | | | |
| | | | | | |
| | | | | | |
| | | | | | |
| | | | | | |
| | | | | | |
| | | | | | |
| | | | | | |
| | | | | | |
| | | | | | |
| | | | | | |
| | | | | | |
| | | | | | |

Based on the information you just completed, which occupations seem to best match your personal characteristics and meet your needs? In the spaces below, you should try to rank your top three options based on their probability of meeting your needs and providing you with career satisfaction and success.

**EXERCISE**

### My Top Three Options:

Option 1: _____

Option 2: _____

Option 3: _____

Now that you have narrowed your options, it is time for the final analysis. Use the Decision-Making Matrix that follows to help you compare your choices. List the three occupations or career alternatives that you are most interested in and the pros and cons associated with each.

## Decision-Making Matrix

Occupation: _____

Pros: _____

_____

Cons: _____

_____

Occupation: _____

Pros: _____

_____

Cons: _____

_____

Occupation: _____

Pros: _____

_____

Cons: _____

_____

---

**EXERCISE**

Now, of the three you listed in the exercise, choose the option that interests you most and appears to have the best chance of meeting your needs and helping you reach your goals:

_____

_____

---

# Step 5: Implement Your Decision

A decision is only that until you act on it and find a way to implement it. Implementing your career decision can mean different things to different people. For some, it will entail using effective job search tools to find the ideal job in which you can fully utilize your full potential; for others, it may mean setting goals to go back to college to earn a degree or an additional degree; and for others, it may mean stepping out on a limb to start a small or home-based business.

> **NOTE**
>
> Remember that your decision is the best one for you at this time. If your needs or interests change later, or if the outcomes of the decision you just made do not seem to take you closer to a rewarding career, you can make a new decision based on new information at that time.

The actions required for this step are much too involved to address in a few paragraphs tacked on to the end of this chapter, which is why the rest of the book will help you through that process.

One thing I know is that the people who are most successful in their lives and their careers are those people who establish long-term career goals that provide future direction and perspective. The good news is that you can develop effective goal-setting and action-planning skills. You must, however, not fear change or worry about failing to achieve your goals. Before moving to the next chapter to develop a career plan, complete the following questions to learn more about how much of a risk-taker you are.

## Taking Calculated Career Risks

Think about the career risks you have taken in the past and then answer the following questions. Doing so will help you uncover your career risk-taking patterns:

What types of career risks do you tend to take most often?

_____

_____

What types of career risks should you take more often?

_____

_____

Are there career risks you should not continue to take?

_____

_____

Do the career risks you take reflect what matters most to you?

_____

_____

# Tying It All Together

Congratulations! You've decided on a career goal—or at least the occupation that will help you meet your career goals. The next step is to create a plan for achieving it. Chapter 8 will help you with the last step in the career decision-making process as you turn your vision for the future into steps to take in the present.

# Plan Your Work–and Work Your Plan

*"Just as collective actions shape society's future, our individual
actions shape our personal destiny."*
*–David Borchard, John Kelly, and Nancy Pat Weaver,*
Your Career: Choices, Chances, and Changes

Carrie is a 27-year-old paralegal who has been working for a large firm in Columbus, Ohio, for the last five years. She has never been married. She graduated from Ohio State University with a degree in sociology. She feels unchallenged and has quickly lost interest in this type of work. She enjoys research, but she does not feel like she helps society in any tangible way.

Carrie says that she has always felt like she would be a good criminal profiler. She has a very analytical mind and took several criminal justice courses while earning her degree, but she does not know how to go about getting this type of job. How should she go about making the transition? How can she best tailor her degree to criminal-profiling positions? Does she need additional education, such as a master's degree? Will she need to get experience as a law enforcement officer? Does that mean she will have to carry a gun? Who has answers to these kinds of questions?

These represent the types of difficult questions that you will probably face if you want a possible career change. (Note the word "types"–most of us aren't worried about having to bring firearms on the job.) You can answer these kinds of questions only through careful planning. Career planning is not an easy process, as you probably found as you tackled the decision making part of it in the last chapter, but it is well worth the time and effort you put into it. Now that you have made some career decisions, it is time to design a plan that will help you reach your goals.

# Taking Responsibility for Your Career

Career planning takes a lot of personal responsibility. It also takes a fair amount of optimism. People who take responsibility for their careers also tend to stay positive. A direct relationship exists between how responsible you are and how much control you feel you have in your life. In turn, a direct relationship also exists between your level of responsibility and the positive emotions you experience. People who feel they have no control, who are victims of fate, or are stuck in their current situation tend to become trapped by negativity, feeling bad for themselves to the point of helplessness.

Your cognitions play a powerful role in how prepared you are to begin the career-planning process. As you learned in the previous chapter, your attitudes can act as stumbling blocks, keeping you from taking action. For example, imagine while driving, you get stuck in traffic due to an accident

> **NOTE**
>
> Unresolved conflicts can sabotage careers and lives. There comes a time when you have to give up negative emotions and stop feeling sorry for yourself. The best way is to stop blaming others for your problems and feelings. Blaming others takes away from your ability to take effective action.

ahead. You will definitely arrive late to that job that you don't really like anyway. You may get mad at the rubbernecking drivers of the cars ahead of you, at the police officers for not showing up faster, or even at the people in the accident. You may dwell on the past and get mad at yourself for not having taken a different route; you may start hoping that you can get a new job with a shorter commute; or you may get mad at your spouse for not having breakfast done quickly enough for you to get on the road sooner. Your internal programming tells you that you need to be somewhere, you are late, and you may even lose your job. Someone, it would seem, is to blame.

But the truth is, you couldn't have predicted the accident. Nor can you predict every change or circumstance that you might face in your career. Blaming yourself or others for what has happened in your career is simply a way to defer the responsibility you need to take from this point on. The question you have to answer isn't, "Who caused me to be stuck in this jam?" but, "What can I do now to get out of it?"

# Goals: Stepping Stones to Achievement

By making a strong commitment to your dreams, you create your own motivation rather than rely on external circumstances to drive you. By committing yourself to a career path, you focus your energy and eliminate indecision. Now you must set purposeful short- and long-term goals to help you maintain your motivation.

Short-term goals describe what you would like to accomplish within the next few months. They act as stepping stones toward the achievement of your long-term goals–those goals you would like to accomplish within the next year or more (sometimes, a lot more). Goals keep you on track. Some people even feel that the journey toward a goal is as important as the goal itself.

## *Defining Your Goals*

Defining your goals is a critical part of reaching them. You can set effective goals by following these guidelines:

- Your goals should be yours, not someone else's.

- Your goals should be stated in as specific, measurable terms as possible.

- Your goals should have observable outcomes so that you know when you have achieved them.

- Your goals should be realistic and attainable.

- You should set specific deadlines for achieving each goal.

- Your goals should be positive and stated positively–focused on what you want to do rather than on what you do not want to do.

Long-term career goals are those that extend far into the future–even as many as 20 or 30 years. These goals may change over time and are the most difficult to achieve. For this reason, you should focus on both short- and long-term goals. Short-term goals tend to be more flexible and more easily achieved. As such, they help provide direction and set guidelines for future action.

The exercise that follows will help you begin to start thinking about what you would like to achieve throughout your career. In the space below, use the guidelines stated above to set some basic career goals. Later in the chapter, you will have the opportunity to revise these initial goals.

| EXERCISE | |
|---|---|
| **Long-Term Goals** | **Short-Term Goals** |
| _____ | _____ |
| _____ | _____ |
| _____ | _____ |
| _____ | _____ |

## *The Art of Accomplishment*

Nicholas Lore, author of the book *The Pathfinder,* sees the career-planning process as the most critical aspect of career success and believes that setting goals is actually the first and most important step in mastering the art of accomplishment. In his art of achievement model, Lore proposes that goals are the engine that actually drives achievement. He contends that you can break down accomplishments into specific cycles of creation, action, and completion. Let's look at each aspect in more detail.

## 1. Creation

In this first phase, you develop ideas of things you would like to do or have. Then, you make a commitment to the ideas and begin to plan how to achieve these goals. In the spaces that follow, list some of the ideas you have and then write a statement of commitment. Be sure to draw on the decision you made in chapter 7 as one possibility.

---

**EXERCISE**

Things I would like to do or have:

_____

_____

_____

How I will commit to achieve these things?

_____

_____

_____

---

## 2. Action

In this second phase, you think about what you need to do to gain the things you would like to do or have.

---

**EXERCISE**

In the space that follows, list some of the things you have to do to get what you want:

_____

_____

_____

---

## 3. Completion

In this third phase, you maintain your energy and enthusiasm until you have accomplished what you set out to achieve. Think about how you will maintain a positive attitude as you work toward your goals.

---

### EXERCISE

How I will maintain my energy and enthusiasm during the completion of my goals?

_____

_____

_____

---

Regardless of the system you use to set and achieve goals, one thing is certain: Setting goals and identifying the steps it takes to achieve them is what career planning is all about. But as with everything else in the career-development process, a career plan is effective only if you approach it with the right attitude. (A good sense of humor might come in handy, too.)

# The Career-Planning Assessment

The following assessment can help you identify your key attitudes about career planning. Read each statement and then decide the extent to which you agree or disagree. Circle one of the four responses to the right of each statement.

- If you strongly believe the statement or feel it is true most of the time, circle the number under **SA (STRONGLY AGREE)**.

- If you believe the statement or feel it is true some of the time, circle the number under **A (AGREE)**.

- If you do not believe the statement or feel it is not true some of the time, circle the number under **D (DISAGREE)**.

- If you strongly do not believe the statement or feel it is not true most of the time, circle the number under **SD (STRONGLY DISAGREE)**.

Of course, there are no right or wrong answers. Be sure to respond to each statement.

|  | SA | A | D | SD |
|---|---|---|---|---|
| 1. I need luck to get ahead in my career | 1 | 2 | 3 | 4 |
| 2. I am interested in learning more about various occupations | 4 | 3 | 2 | 1 |
| 3. I am flexible when considering career options | 4 | 3 | 2 | 1 |
| 4. I have developed long-term career goals | 4 | 3 | 2 | 1 |
| 5. I feel like I cannot get ahead in this world | 1 | 2 | 3 | 4 |
| 6. I have talked with a career counselor about my career options | 4 | 3 | 2 | 1 |

_(continued)_

*(continued)*

| | SA | A | D | SD |
|---|---|---|---|---|
| 7. I am always looking for new career opportunities | 4 | 3 | 2 | 1 |
| 8. My long-term goals are too hard to achieve | 1 | 2 | 3 | 4 |
| 9. It is futile to plan for my career | 1 | 2 | 3 | 4 |
| 10. I have observed workers in occupations of interest to me | 4 | 3 | 2 | 1 |
| 11. I have little or no choice in what career to pursue | 1 | 2 | 3 | 4 |
| 12. Career planning can be an exciting process | 4 | 3 | 2 | 1 |
| 13. I have read materials to learn more about the world of work | 4 | 3 | 2 | 1 |
| 14. I usually take the first job available to me | 1 | 2 | 3 | 4 |
| 15. Setting goals is critical for career success | 4 | 3 | 2 | 1 |
| 16. Life is full of choices | 4 | 3 | 2 | 1 |
| 17. I am willing to spend the time and effort needed to choose the best occupation for me | 4 | 3 | 2 | 1 |
| 18. Some occupations are for men and others are for women | 1 | 2 | 3 | 4 |
| 19. I know how to set career goals | 4 | 3 | 2 | 1 |
| 20. Others know better what type of work is best for me | 1 | 2 | 3 | 4 |
| 21. I am aware of the educational requirements for occupations that interest me | 4 | 3 | 2 | 1 |
| 22. I am interested in talking to people in different occupations | 4 | 3 | 2 | 1 |
| 23. It is important to investigate all options and alternatives before making decisions | 4 | 3 | 2 | 1 |
| 24. People should just wait for the right job opportunity to come along | 1 | 2 | 3 | 4 |
| 25. I have many different career options | 4 | 3 | 2 | 1 |
| 26. People should consider all possibilities and then choose the best available option | 4 | 3 | 2 | 1 |
| 27. Career problems are challenges to be solved | 4 | 3 | 2 | 1 |
| 28. People should be involved in their own career development | 4 | 3 | 2 | 1 |
| 29. Having a lot of career possibilities makes me nervous | 1 | 2 | 3 | 4 |
| 30. I always set specific and achievable goals | 4 | 3 | 2 | 1 |

**Total:** _____

## Scoring

This assessment measures your attitude concerning career development and career planning and helps you identify possible barriers to that process. Count the total raw score of the items you circled. Transfer your total score to the space below:

**Career-Planning Total:** _____

A score from 91—120 means that you are ready to take an active role in the career-planning process. A score from 30—59, on the other hand, means some mental or attitudinal barriers stand in the way of your career planning.

Your attitude determines your ability to develop a sound career plan. The lower your score, the less likely you are to take charge of your career. People who do not prepare to take responsibility for their careers tend to be at the mercy of forces outside of themselves. They take whatever jobs come their way and do not actively initiate the career changes necessary for greater career and life satisfaction. They are ships tossed around in the stormy seas of career inertia, stuck without a map or a paddle, waiting for the next wave to come.

The following sections can help you take more responsibility for your career development. While this is especially important for anyone who scored in the low or average range on the preceding assessment, just about anyone can benefit from a little extra career-planning advice.

# The Four Characteristics of Effective Career Planners

Effective career plans come from good career planners. Researchers and career theorists have identified several characteristics that effective career planners have in common. Regardless of your score on the assessment in this chapter, keep the following characteristics in mind as you complete your own career-planning process.

## Career Planners Are Active

People who are good at career planning are actively invested in the process and do not rely on other people to make plans for them. People who are active identify career choices that are unique and appropriate to them rather than passively accept the choices offered by others or that are easy or readily available. They trust in their own ability to make career decisions. They see problems in their lives as challenges that they can solve, and they proactively set out to make positive changes rather than wait for outside forces to impose changes on them.

Use the following worksheet to assess your own active role in the career-planning process and what you can do to become more active.

---

**I am not confident in making career decisions.**

Reasons for inactivity: _____

Why or why not? _____

What I can do about it: _____

**I blame other people when I make bad decisions.**

Reasons for inactivity: _____

Why or why not? _____

What I can do about it: _____

**I am passive in making career decisions.**

Reasons for inactivity: _____

Why or why not? _____

What I can do about it: _____

**I do not like making career decisions.**

Reasons for inactivity: _____

Why or why not? _____

What I can do about it: _____

---

# Career Planners Are Involved

People who are good at career planning become highly involved in the whole process. They commit and motivate themselves to explore career options and gather career-related information. They see career development as a lifelong process of decision making, implementation, and adjustment. They discuss their careers with knowledgeable people, family, and friends and will put in hours at the library or engage in job shadowing or informational interviewing to learn as much as they can about their options. They see all things as somehow relating to their career development and truly believe that careful research and planning will pay off in the form of a more satisfying career.

Use the following worksheet to assess your involvement in the career-planning process and what you can do to become more involved.

---

**I am not interested in researching career information.**

Reasons for not being involved: _____

Why or why not? _____

How I can become more involved: _____

**I think that career decisions are irreversible.**

Reasons for not being involved: _____

Why or why not? _____

How I can become more involved: _____

**I do not want to discuss my career with friends, family, or a career counselor.**

Reasons for not being involved: _____

Why or why not? _____

How I can become more involved: _____

**I have trouble seeing how all parts of my life are related to my career.**

Reasons for not being involved: _____

Why or why not? _____

How I can become more involved: _____

**I am not willing to commit the time, effort, and energy necessary to plan my career.**

Reasons for not being involved: _____

Why or why not? _____

How I can become more involved: _____

---

# *Career Planners Make Compromises*

People who are good at career planning are willing to compromise. This isn't to suggest that they sacrifice their dreams or desires–only that they are flexible in considering all the career options available to them. They continuously look for new opportunities and can realistically appraise their career options based on knowledge about themselves and about the world of work. Most importantly, they understand the need to make informed decisions based on carefully calculated risks, and they also understand that career development is a process.

## NOTE

In making career decisions and plans, you will have to make some sacrifices. The key is to prioritize your wants and needs and then plan a career that satisfies as many of them as possible. The job that pays a hundred grand a year may only come with two weeks of paid vacation–but with that kind of salary, those could be some spectacular vacations.

Use the following worksheet to assess your openness to compromise in the career-planning process and what you can do to become more flexible.

---

**EXERCISE**

**I am rarely open to new career opportunities.**

Reasons for not compromising: _____

Why or why not? _____

How I can become more open to compromise: _____

**I am stuck in my current line of work.**

Reasons for not compromising: _____

Why or why not? _____

How I can become more open to compromise: _____

**I lack knowledge about myself and the world of work.**

Reasons for not compromising: _____

Why or why not? _____

How I can become more open to compromise: _____

**I believe that only one perfect job exists for me.**

Reasons for not compromising: _____

Why or why not? _____

How I can become more open to compromise: _____

---

# Career Planners Are Goal Oriented

People who are good at career planning are goal oriented; they willingly establish career goals and enthusiastically pursue them. They take responsibility for developing their careers. They use short-term goals as benchmarks to stay motivated toward reaching their long-term goals. They initiate career changes much more effectively, constantly reviewing and revising their goals to meet their current needs.

Use the following worksheet to assess how goal oriented you are and what you can do to become more goal oriented.

---

**EXERCISE**

**I do not take responsibility for developing my own career.**

Reasons for not being goal oriented: _____

Why or why not? _____

How I can become more goal oriented: _____

**I have no or limited short-term goals.**

Reasons for not being goal oriented: _____

Why or why not? _____

How I can become more goal oriented: _____

**I have no or limited long-term goals.**

Reasons for not being goal oriented: _____

Why or why not? _____

How I can become more goal oriented: _____

**I have difficulty implementing my career goals.**

Reasons for not being goal oriented: _____

Why or why not? _____

How I can become more goal oriented: _____

---

# Developing Your Career Plan

Now that you have chosen an occupation to pursue, you might feel tempted to sit back and wait for the recruiter to knock down your door and welcome you to your chosen profession.

This will definitely not happen (even if you have a flimsy door). As the quote that opens the chapter tells us, our actions shape our destiny. Now is the time for you to roll up your sleeves and get to work to develop the specific career goals that will make up your career plan.

You can break down your career dreams into specific goals with realistic completion dates. Those goals are the bridge to get you where you want to be. In the previous chapter, you identified an occupation that you would like to pursue. Begin by making it the focus of your career goals by listing it below:

**My Current Career Choice:** _____

While your overall career goal may be to become a "fill in the blank here," it's important to realize that this goal consists of several smaller goals or related goals. For example, if your occupational choice is "firefighter," that, in turn, requires you to meet other career goals–you will need to train for, enroll in, and pass a firefighter training program and examination. If your occupational choice was "actor," you may have multiple goals to work toward, from enrolling in acting school to landing a lead role in a local production to finding an agent.

The next steps will help you define clear and measurable career goals and then identify and overcome potential barriers to completing them. Just remember that attitude is key. You must become active, involved, and willing to make compromises if you want to achieve those goals and establish your dream career.

# Step 1: Define Your Goals

The first step in setting and reaching effective career goals is to define them so that they are realistic and achievable. Take a look at some sample career goals:

- Be successful.

- Make a lot of money.

- Be happy at work.

- Be a good leader.

Notice that these career goals are vague and difficult to measure. When you develop career goals, remember that the goals should have the following characteristics: specific, measurable, attainable, relevant to you, and tied to a timeline. Let's take a look at each characteristic in more detail:

- **Specific:** Goals must be stated in concrete, behavioral terms. For example, "I would like to start my own advertising agency in Pittsburgh within the next six months" would be a concrete, behavioral goal.

- **Measurable:** Goals must be assessable so that you can track your progress. For example, "Earning a bachelor's degree in nursing" is measurable, whereas "Getting educated" is not.

- **Attainable:** Goals must be within your reach, or you will not be motivated to work toward them. You must feel as though you have a realistic opportunity to achieve your goals; for example, feeling as though you have the time, patience, and intelligence to earn a bachelor's degree (not to mention the money).

- **Relevant:** Goals must be important in your overall career plan; for example, knowing that attaining a bachelor's degree will help you get a promotion or better job.

- **Timed:** Goals must have deadlines attached to them if you want them to motivate you, although you need to be reasonable and set deadlines that you can realistically commit to; for example, earning a bachelor's degree within the next five years (which is how long it takes most people nowadays).

Let's follow Katie as she sets some career goals. Katie works as a shipping clerk for a large manufacturing company. She makes approximately $30,000 a year and would like to rise to a leadership position within the corporation. Notice some of the career goals that she sets for herself:

- "Return to college to work on my degree in business administration. I will finish my degree within the next five years."

- "Find a job that pays at least $45,000 a year after I complete my bachelor's degree."

- "Ask one of my coworkers to be my mentor. I need to accomplish this by the end of next month."

- "Ask my supervisor if I can take on a greater leadership role with the corporation. I need to do this within the next two weeks."

Notice that all the above goals are specific, realistic, measurable, and achievable and that time-frames are given for each.

Now take some time to define your own goals. Goals should be positively stated, be realistic, identify specific behaviors, and be within your ability to achieve them. Use the space below to set four or more career goals related to the occupation that interests you most.

---

**EXERCISE**

My career goals:

_____

_____

_____

---

# Step 2: Rank Your Goals

The next step is to rank your goals into short- and long-term goals. Most people need to achieve their short-term goals before their long-terms goals. Remember that short-term goals are career objectives that you would like to achieve in a year or less. On the other hand, long-term goals are career objectives that you want to achieve over a longer period of time and can be set 5 to 10 years into the future. Look how Katie sorts her goals:

**Short-term goals:**

- "Ask one of my coworkers to be my mentor. I need to accomplish this by the end of next month."

- "Ask my supervisor if I can take on a greater leadership role with the corporation. I need to do this within the next two weeks."

**Long-term goals:**

- "Return to college to work on my degree in business administration. I will finish my degree within the next five years."

- "Find a job that pays at least $45,000 a year after I complete my bachelor's degree."

Use the space below to categorize your goals into short- and long-term goals.

| EXERCISE | |
| --- | --- |
| **Short-Term Goals** | **Long-Term Goals** |
| _____ | _____ |
| _____ | _____ |
| _____ | _____ |

# Step 3: Identify Roadblocks to Your Goals

Next, you will need to identify people, circumstances, or other barriers that might prevent you from achieving your career goals. For Katie, some of these roadblocks might include the following:

**"Ask one of my coworkers to be my mentor."**

- Identifying a person whom I think will be a good career mentor
- Gathering the courage to ask someone to be my mentor
- Working out an agenda for the mentoring process

**"Ask my supervisor if I can take on a greater leadership role with the corporation."**

- Effectively communicating my interest in leadership activities to my supervisor
- Identifying problems I could solve
- Proving to my supervisor that I deserve the opportunity

**"Return to college to work on my degree in business administration."**

- Exploring whether I can return college
- Improving my study habits
- Finding a way to pay for classes
- Determining whether business administration is the best degree for me to pursue
- Identifying a college in my area
- Being accepted to the college
- Finding time to take classes

**"Find a job that pays at least $45,000 a year."**

- Completing my college degree
- Rebuilding my resume to show off my accomplishments

- Building a network of potential employers

- Enhancing my leadership skills

- Joining professional organizations that can help me in my search for a new job

As you can see, it will take much more time and effort for Katie to accomplish her long-term goals. However, accomplishing her short-term goals will help her build confidence. For example, taking a leadership role in her current company will enhance her managerial skills, which in turn will make her more marketable when she looks for a job with her new degree.

Use the worksheet below to identify obstacles that might prevent you from achieving your career goals. For each goal, identify the potential roadblocks to your achievement.

| EXERCISE | |
|---|---|
| **Short-Term Goals** | **Potential Roadblocks** |
| _____ | _____ |
| _____ | _____ |
| _____ | _____ |
| **Long-Term Goals** | **Potential Roadblocks** |
| _____ | _____ |
| _____ | _____ |
| _____ | _____ |

# Step 4: Overcome Your Roadblocks

This last step is the action stage–the opportunity to work toward achieving your goals. You will need to develop a strategy or step-by-step process that will help you overcome your roadblocks. For Katie, some of those strategies might include the following:

- Asking to manage special projects at work

- Exploring financial aid options with a loan officer

- Taking assessments to determine her interest, skills, and abilities

- Researching alternative ways to take classes, such as through distance-learning programs

- Joining professional business management organizations

- Networking with supervisors in her city

There are hundreds of other ways Katie can overcome her roadblocks. Also, as Katie achieves some of her short-term goals, new ones will present themselves–with new complications requiring new strategies. This is the nature of career development. It is an ongoing, multistep process, which is precisely why it requires a plan.

Use the worksheet below to explore proactive things you can do to overcome roadblocks to your career goals.

---

**EXERCISE**

**Roadblocks to Short-Term Goals**          **Ways I Will Overcome Them**

_____          _____

_____          _____

_____          _____

**Roadblocks to Long-Term Goals**          **Ways I Will Overcome Them**

_____          _____

_____          _____

_____          _____

---

Congratulations! You have learned more about your career-planning skills and have successfully developed career goals and a career plan for achieving these goals. Remember that you must remain active in this process, revise and change goals as new opportunities present themselves, and stick to the deadlines you have set for yourself.

# Tying It All Together

Remember that your attitude about career planning is extremely important when looking for your ideal job and developing a successful career. In addition to a positive attitude, generating an effective career plan also requires skills in setting goals and implementation. Many people are reluctant to set goals or develop any type of plan for fear that they will not stay committed to them and fail. That's why it's important to remember that your goals should provide you with direction and motivation and that you can, and will, make changes as you encounter new situations and meet new people.

In the next chapter, you will continue the career-planning process by learning how to effectively balance work and leisure in your career.

# CHAPTER 9

# Keep Your Balance

*"The best and safest thing is to keep a balance in your life....*
*If you can do that, and live that way, you are really a wise man."*
*—Euripides*

My wife, Kathy, loves to work. She never complains about having to get up in the mornings and never dreads Sunday evenings, knowing that another workweek is about to begin. She willingly brings work home and rarely takes vacation days. She enjoys climbing the corporate ladder. Even when she does have leisure time, she usually thinks about the different projects she has to do. Sometimes, she even feels guilty for taking time off. If we won the lottery, Kathy would continue to work as if nothing had happened.

Personally, I think she's nuts.

I tend to be just the opposite. I love my idle hours–time for fun, relaxation, and personal exploration. I could spend hours playing chess, writing, playing with my dog, volunteering at church, or simply sitting on my back porch. I never feel guilty for having leisure time on my hands. I do not like too much responsibility, and I want to leave the office at five and not have to think about my job until the next morning. I have no interest in corporate ladder climbing. If we won the lottery, I would quit work the next day, clicking my heels as I walked out the door.

Neither my wife nor I do a great job of balancing work and leisure, and we aren't alone. The work-leisure balance can be one of the most difficult aspects of managing a career. But without that balance, people can end up addicted to one or the other. My wife and I try to help each other gain more work-leisure balance, but it is easy to fall back into old habits and favor one role in your career development to the exclusion of others.

This chapter will help you explore how effectively you balance your work and leisure roles–and learn some more effective ways to balance them better to make your career and your life more satisfying. As you plan your career and even as you search for your next job, you should always keep your need for balance in mind.

# Balancing Work and Leisure

Workers across the world–and Americans especially–have a difficult time balancing work and leisure, in part because the pressures of work have intensified. Studies of workplace trends suggest that for many people, the demands of work dominate life. This, in turn, has prompted claims that the quality of life, career satisfaction, and our sense of community have started to deteriorate.

Much of this pressure comes from the top down. Many corporate employers demand that employees work longer hours, take work home, work weekends, and take less vacation time, forcing those employees to choose between work and leisure. In contrast, many new employees desire more balance between work and the rest of their lives. They don't want to provide unlimited and unconditional commitment to their jobs. In fact, recent research shows that many of the young adults entering the workforce willingly sacrifice money for time, taking lower salaries in favor of more vacations or the ability to work from home.

---

**LEISURE DEFINED**

Career theorists have defined *leisure* in many ways. Some have called it a state of being or a condition of the soul. Others consider it as any activity viewed as less important than work. Still others define leisure as any activity engaged in by choice (suggesting, and rightly so for many people, that work is *not* a matter of choice). To be sure, the definitions have changed considerably over time and differ from one culture to the next.

For the purposes of this book, leisure is any self-determined activity or experience that you aren't paid for–made possible because you have time or income to spare.

---

Many people lead unbalanced lives, engaging in work *or* leisure to the exclusion of the other. As with most things, living in either extreme–workaholism or leisure addiction–can have unhealthy consequences. Achieving the proper work-life balance means having sufficient time to commit to activities at both work and home. The result of achieving such balance is greater life satisfaction and greater career success. The career decisions you make should always take your need for this balance into account. Otherwise, you might find yourself making those decisions over and over again until you find the right balance.

# Your Career Is a Combination

Remember that your career is a combination of your work and other life roles that together express your total pattern of self-development. In other words, your career is more than just what you do for a living. It's who you are and how you develop. It's the goals you set and your path to achieving them.

Thus, your career is a combination of your work roles and your leisure roles. Carl McDaniels was one of the first career development professionals to show an interest in how work and leisure combine to form a career. He suggested that "Career equals work plus leisure." Thus, those who focus solely on work or solely on leisure miss out on a crucial piece of the equation. As a result, their career simply won't add up.

For you to be happy and live a life that is (mostly) free of stress, you need to be able to balance the two. Research has determined that a balanced combination of job satisfaction and leisure satisfaction is one of the primary predictors of physical and psychological health. Job satisfaction alone is not enough.

In fact, for many people, leisure is the *antidote* to a lack of job satisfaction. One way that leisure can help people who are bored or lack meaning and satisfaction at work is through *compensation*. People who are unfulfilled at work can make up for it through hobbies and activities that satisfy the needs not being met on the job.

Take Jerry, for example. Jerry works as a plumber in Pittsburgh, following in his father's footsteps. He likes the work well enough and is well-paid. His real passion, however, is photography. Photography allows him to express his creative side, something he isn't really able to do on the job (most people prefer that their plumbers *not* get creative). He hopes one day to make a living selling his photographs. Until then, Jerry gains enough satisfaction from taking pictures as a hobby that he does not mind fixing pipes. Like Jerry, the less you can satisfy your needs at work, the more you must rely on leisure-time activities for your life satisfaction.

Ultimately, the relationship between your work and leisure–and the effects of the balance (or imbalance) between the two–can take a variety of forms:

- **Separation:** Your work and leisure are two distinct facets of your life that do not influence each other. While possible, it is hard to imagine that the time put into work and the money earned from it have no impact on your hobbies or interests–or that leisure activities have no effect on your work life. True separation is quite difficult to manage.

- **Spillover:** Little or no distinction exists between your work and leisure. You find so much satisfaction engaging in one activity that you choose to do it in both your work and free time. Imagine a veterinarian who loves working with animals so much that she volunteers at the local animal shelter on the weekends or a video game designer who plays Xbox in his free time.

- **Compensation:** You can compensate what you lack in one area of life by engaging in activities in another area. For example, someone who dislikes her desk job shuffling papers because it is too stationary and predictable may enjoy mountain climbing on the weekends.

- **Conflict:** High levels of demand in one area of life can cause conflicts in the other. Such conflicts are frequent and are often part of the career management process (although with more *careful* management, you can avoid them). A person who works too much may experience difficulties at home with family members–a common complaint among workers who feel the pressure to put their careers first.

Recognizing the patterns that your work and leisure take, how they interact, and the effects that interaction has on your well-being is important. Knowing the balance you need to strike can help you develop a career plan that is right for you.

# The Work-Leisure Balance Scale

The following assessment measures your orientation and commitment to work and leisure. In other words, it helps you see where you fall on the work-leisure continuum and just how balanced you are. Read each item carefully to decide how much you agree with that statement. For each choice listed, circle the number of your response on the line to the right. There are no right or wrong answers. Be sure to respond to each item by circling the response that best describes you.

|  | Always True | Very True | Somewhat True | Not True |
|---|---|---|---|---|
| 1. I do not have much of a social life because I am always working | 4 | 3 | 2 | 1 |
| 2. My job consumes too much of my time as it is | 1 | 2 | 3 | 4 |
| 3. I rarely bring work home with me | 1 | 2 | 3 | 4 |
| 4. I often feel I must drop everything else for my work | 4 | 3 | 2 | 1 |
| 5. I have lots of hobbies | 1 | 2 | 3 | 4 |
| 6. I feel like I can never finish my work | 4 | 3 | 2 | 1 |
| 7. I am not very goal oriented | 1 | 2 | 3 | 4 |
| 8. Leisure time is just time off to rest up for work | 4 | 3 | 2 | 1 |
| 9. I am driven to perform well at work | 4 | 3 | 2 | 1 |
| 10. I often do work-related jobs in my spare time | 4 | 3 | 2 | 1 |
| 11. I need the structure of work in my life | 4 | 3 | 2 | 1 |
| 12. I judge myself by my accomplishments | 4 | 3 | 2 | 1 |
| 13. I like to be in total control of situations at work | 4 | 3 | 2 | 1 |
| 14. I am not worried about advancing at work | 1 | 2 | 3 | 4 |
| 15. I often take on additional responsibilities | 4 | 3 | 2 | 1 |
| 16. I am interested only in the results of my work | 4 | 3 | 2 | 1 |
| 17. I rarely obsess over work to be done | 1 | 2 | 3 | 4 |
| 18. I often work as many as 12 hours each day | 4 | 3 | 2 | 1 |

|  | Always True | Very True | Somewhat True | Not True |
|---|---|---|---|---|
| 19. I rarely work evenings and weekends | 1 | 2 | 3 | 4 |
| 20. I like to take days off | 4 | 3 | 2 | 1 |
| 21. I am often unable to relax after work | 4 | 3 | 2 | 1 |
| 22. I am constantly thinking about work | 4 | 3 | 2 | 1 |
| 23. I feel guilty when I am not working | 4 | 3 | 2 | 1 |
| 24. I cannot wait for the next vacation or holiday | 1 | 2 | 3 | 4 |
| 25. I spend my free time doing activities not related to work | 1 | 2 | 3 | 4 |
| 26. I get bored when I am not working | 4 | 3 | 2 | 1 |
| 27. I come into work even if I am sick | 4 | 3 | 2 | 1 |
| 28. I cope with life's problems by working harder | 4 | 3 | 2 | 1 |
| 29. I would quit my job if I did not need the money | 1 | 2 | 3 | 4 |
| 30. I do not know what to do with my time off | 4 | 3 | 2 | 1 |

## Scoring

Add up the scores you circled for each item on the assessment. Then, transfer your total to the space below:

**Work-Leisure Balance Total:** _____

Now put an *X* on the line indicating your total score for the assessment.

←30 | | 45 | | 60 | | 75 | | 90 | | 105 | | 120→

Leisure Lover          Balanced          Workaholic

# Exploring Your Work-Leisure Balance

We all define success differently. How you define success depends on what you value in life and in your career. Some people value work above all, and some people value leisure. The majority of people value some combination of the two. In essence, your lifestyle is what you need and value in relation to work and leisure in your life, and your career is the path you take to create that lifestyle.

Look at your work-leisure balance total. Totals from 91—120 are high and indicate a *work orientation,* a person that is generally more interested in work than leisure. Especially high scores may indicate tendencies toward workaholism. By contrast, scores from 30—60 are

> **NOTE**
>
> Perhaps you are already perfectly content with your balance of work and leisure. But that doesn't mean it will stay in balance forever. The exercises that follow can also give you some tips for maintaining the balance you've already achieved.

low and indicate a *leisure orientation,* a person that privileges his or her leisure activities and is not willing to sacrifice them for work. Especially low scores may suggest a lack of motivation to succeed at work. As you might expect, scores from 61—90 indicate a *balanced orientation.*

Read about your orientation on the following pages and then complete the exercises that follow. This will help you develop a keener sense of how to balance your work life with the rest of your life, which in turn can lead to smarter career choices and better career management.

# *Work Orientation*

People with a work orientation see their jobs as their greatest (and sometimes only) source of life satisfaction. They work long hours and devote much of their energy to their jobs, sometimes even preferring work to spending time with family and friends. As a consequence, they perform well in demanding jobs. Leisure may be important in their lives but only after all their work is done. They are very results oriented and will often work extra hours to complete projects. They need work that is challenging, that allows them to set goals, and that lets them measure their achievement. They often feel guilty when not working. Some might say they are addicted to the work they do.

## All Work and No Play: The Dangers of Workaholism

Some people live for their work. It is second only to oxygen on their list of daily requirements. Such people might be considered "workaholics." Research estimates that millions of people in the workforce suffer from workaholism, a progressive disease in which you become addicted to the process of working. Working gives such people a "high" and becomes something they depend on. Workaholics ultimately develop a rationalization for why they have to work so hard. Like other types of addicts, they are in denial about their obsession and compulsion with work. The following statistics give a little insight into how Americans especially tend to gravitate toward this extreme:

- Overall, employees in the United States earn fewer vacation days than any other country in the industrialized world. People in the United States earn an average of 13 days per year for vacations. In Japan, employees earn 25 days per year, while in Italy, employees earn 42 days per year.

- Overall, employees in the United States work more than employees in any other country in the industrialized world. In the United States, an employee now averages approximately 50 hours per week. By comparison, in most other countries in the world, the workweek is limited to 45 hours per week, while the official workweek in France has been reduced to 35 hours per week.

- In the United States, workaholism adversely affects more than one million employees per year.

> ### WORKING YOURSELF TO DEATH
>
> Although the term "workaholic" is not yet an official medical or psychological diagnosis, the compulsion to work can have detrimental effects on your life and career. In Japan, it is called *Karoshi*, or "death by overwork," and causes approximately 1,000 deaths per year, accounting for nearly 5 percent of the country's stroke and heart attack victims in employees under the age of 60.

What makes *workaholism* different from *hard work* is the obsession. For the workaholic, the desire to work is all encompassing. Even when they do something social or engage in a hobby, the workaholic cannot concentrate for thinking about work. As a result, a workaholic's life continues to revolve around his or her job, and all other areas of his or her life become affected, including physical health, social relationships, domestic life, and leisure time.

Some common problems associated with workaholism include a disruption in family life, marital problems, an increase in stress-related diseases, job burnout, and an increase in poor health. Workaholics are the people who miss important events like soccer games and school plays because they feel they must work. Workaholics have nothing else to balance their lives–no hobbies, no leisure activities, no community activities, and no spiritual connections–with potentially devastating results. As the saying goes, all work and no play can make Jack...well...dead–or at least high strung, exhausted, and a prime candidate for blood-pressure medication.

## How the Work Oriented Find Balance

Ernie Zelinski, in his book *The Joy of Not Working*, pointed out the differences at work between a workaholic and one who balances work and leisure:

| Workaholic | Balanced Performer |
|---|---|
| Works long hours | Works regular hours |
| Has no defined goals–works to be active | Has defined goals–works toward objectives |
| Cannot delegate work | Delegates as much as possible |
| Has no interests outside work | Has many interests outside work |
| Misses vacations to work | Takes and enjoys vacations |
| Develops acquaintances at work | Develops deep friendships outside work |
| Always talks about work | Minimizes talk about work |
| Feels life is difficult | Feels life is a celebration |

People with a work orientation tend to spend too much time and effort engaged in work-related activities. Thus, one of the best ways to achieve balance is to identify fulfilling leisure-time activities. One of the most important benefits of leisure is its ability to reduce stress and help you stop thinking about work so much.

The important thing is to find hobbies and activities that are different from your work but that still appeal to your interests. One person's leisure activity is another person's version of "just more work," whether it's jogging, baking, reading novels, or volunteering at the local animal shelter. The key is to engage in these activities because you *want to*–because they fill needs that your work can't–not because you think you *should*.

Answering the following questions can help you become more balanced in your approach to work and leisure:

---

### EXERCISE

What needs do you have that are not met by your work (revisit chapter 2 for some ideas)?

_____

_____

How do your leisure activities fulfill your needs?

_____

_____

How can you find more time for leisure?

_____

_____

What new leisure activities would you explore if you had more time?

_____

_____

---

In addition to simply choosing and engaging in your favorite leisure activities, other things can help you have a more balanced career and life. Consider the following as you seek balance:

- **Time for relationships:** It is important that you take time each day to connect with important people in your life. This may mean scheduling this time (actually writing it in a calendar or planner) until you begin to adopt it as a permanent part of your day.

- **Time alone:** Take time for yourself. Use it to reflect and recharge. If you know how, try meditating for an hour a day. Meditation can help you focus on the moment and stop thinking about work that needs to be done in the future.

- **Breaks:** You can easily build breaks into your work schedule. Even if you have been working quite well without taking breaks, you probably have not experienced your optimum level of creativity, motivation, and energy. Almost all employers allow for some breaks during the day.

- **Exercise:** Exercise has been shown to be an excellent stress-buster. People who exercise regularly tend to be happier, are more energetic, and have a better outlook on life.

- **Vacations:** Use your vacation time for rest and relaxation. Of course, everyone has a different idea about what constitutes rest and relaxation. My wife and I love international vacations with lots of sightseeing. Our neighbors prefer to rent a cabin on the lake only an hour out of town. Commit to using your vacation days (don't try to carry them over without a great reason for doing so) and find a restful way to spend them.

## *Leisure Orientation*

Individuals with a leisure orientation privilege other life activities over their work. Work is a necessity–a means to an end. It provides them with the resources required to engage in hobbies or activities, spend time with their family, or accomplish other life goals. They have little interest in jobs that consume too much of their time and energy. They meet their needs for self-esteem and self-actualization through their hobbies, community activities, and leisure experiences. Some might even see this preference for leisure as a sign of laziness or a lack of drive.

> **NOTE**
>
> Traditional thinking on careers often does not account for "play," instead measuring the success of a career by the extrinsic rewards it affords. Work is work. Careers are made up of jobs, and jobs are not supposed to be "fun." But work can be enjoyable if it allows people to engage in activities that interest them and lets them be interactive, spontaneous, and creative.

### All Play and No Work: The Drawbacks of Leisure Addiction

People who engage in leisure to the exclusion of work tend to have their own problems at work and at home. Leisure-lovers tend to be unpredictable employees. They are often just motivated enough to do a passable job (enough to avoid getting fired) but not a great job (enough to avoid getting promoted). Leisure-lovers work primarily to pay for their leisure-time experiences. Therefore, their commitment to the organization and to coworkers tends to be less intense. While they usually do not experience much stress associated with work, their lack of a more balanced work ethic can have drastic long-term effects on their careers.

### THE EVER-SHIFTING BALANCE

Naturally, our leisure activities change as we grow older, and inevitably, the balance shifts. The chances of us becoming workaholics as toddlers or even teenagers is less likely than when we are in our 30s. Likewise, it may shift again as we near retirement and seek more time for leisure to make up for the loss of a work role. While the balance shifts, the importance of incorporating leisure into career development never diminishes.

If you do not invest enough time and effort in your job, you will lack career focus and career direction. Work provides structure and needed financial rewards for you and your family. Besides the money, work meets many of your other needs, including a place to go, a social network, a sense of self-esteem, and a sense of belonging. All play and no work can leave Jack feeling lost, empty, and unfulfilled.

## How the Leisure-Oriented Find Balance

We all need balance, and working is a part of maintaining that balance. Ideally, you will want to find work related to your leisure-time interests or at least find work that you enjoy as much as these interests.

Answering the following questions can help you become more balanced in your approach to work and leisure.

---

**EXERCISE**

In your work, what are your aspirations and ambitions?

_____

_____

What part does family play in your balanced-life approach?

_____

_____

In your leisure time, how do you meet the following needs?

   Companionship: _____

   Self-esteem: _____

   Creativity: _____

How could you begin to meet these needs at work?

_____

_____

How could your leisure interests help you achieve your career goals?

_____

_____

---

# *Balanced Orientation*

People with a balanced orientation can meet their needs and find life and career satisfaction through a variety of work and leisure activities. They have a healthy work ethic and enjoy their work but use their leisure time to rejuvenate and pursue other interests. They want to be good at what they do, but they are not obsessed with their work.

## Staying Balanced

For those of you who are experiencing a balanced orientation, congratulations, but realize that you still have your work (and leisure) cut out for you. As your life becomes more complex and you experience increasing demands on your time, maintaining that balance becomes more difficult–and even more important.

Most people strive for a balanced orientation, but few achieve it. Many of us feel overwhelmed trying to juggle jobs, family, children's activities, leisure activities, community responsibilities, and school. It is no surprise that work–because it fills many of our needs, especially the most basic ones–can dominate. Here are some things to keep in mind as you work to maintain the balance in your career:

> **NOTE**
>
> As you begin to walk the career path you've outlined in previous chapters, be sure to keep your balance. If you happen to fall down, pull yourself back up and think about what you can do to regain that balance before moving forward again.

- Be aware of things happening in the moment.

- Continue to engage in satisfying work and leisure activities.

- Review and alter (if need be) your definition of success. Consider what you believe about work and leisure, and be sure to remember that leisure is a worthwhile pursuit in your life and your career.

- Take vacations that you enjoy and that allow you to feel rested and rejuvenated.

- Whether in your work or leisure-time activities, be sure to pursue your passions. Identify what you really enjoy doing and then find an outlet to do it.

- Know that you can complete your personal mission or calling in life in your work role, in your leisure role, or in both.

Take some time to reflect on ways that you can maintain your balance as you make your career transition and plan your next career move.

---

### EXERCISE

Things I am currently doing or can start doing to maintain my work-leisure balance:

_____

_____

_____

# Tying It All Together

As a balance of work and leisure, your career encompasses all the roles you come to play during the course of your life. Of course, the length of these roles and how many you engage in at one time will vary depending on your situation. For example, a person who is not married will not play the spouse role but may compensate by engaging in the citizen role more than someone who is. Of course, the more roles you have to play, the less time and money you have to allocate to each role. A wife and mother of two who works as a nurse, lobbies for animal rights, and runs her own scrap-booking club will constantly face the challenge of balancing each role and making career decisions based on her need to keep or shift that balance.

The balance between work and leisure is one of the most critical issues confronting today's worker. As you develop your career plan, remember to take into account *all* the roles you play in life. You must find a balance that is right for you and your situation. By making balance a priority, you have taken another step toward achieving greater career satisfaction, which, in turn, can lead to greater success.

The worksheet that follows can help you summarize everything you've learned about yourself in this part of the book. From there, it is on to the last stage in the career-planning process (and the last part of this book): taking action to make your career dreams come true.

# Part III Summary: Develop a Career Plan

In this section, you have identified potential barriers to your career decision making and development and identified strategies for making more effective decisions. You have also set career goals and begun to formulate a plan to reach them. Finally, you have identified where you stand in terms of balancing your work and leisure and explored strategies for staying in balance as you continue to develop your career. The next step is to put your plan into action.

Based on the results of the assessments and the information you completed in each chapter, use the following worksheet to summarize what you've discovered about yourself. You can then use this information to further develop and assess your career plan. By pulling together your results from all three chapters, you should have a much better sense of what steps you need to take to achieve career success and satisfaction.

---

### EXERCISE

My barriers to effective career decision making (from chapter 7):

_____

_____

Ways I can overcome those barriers:

_____

_____

The career decision I've made: _____

My attitude toward career development (from chapter 8):

_____

_____

Ways that I can become more active and invested in my own career development:

_____

_____

---

*(continued)*

*(continued)*

My work-leisure orientation (from chapter 9): _____

Ways I can better balance my work and leisure roles:

_____

_____

_____

What steps can I take immediately to pursue my chosen career goal?

_____

_____

_____

# PART IV: TAKE ACTION

*"There are risks and costs to a program of action. But they are far less than the long-range risks and costs of comfortable inaction."*
—John F. Kennedy

# CHAPTER 10

# Improve Your Job Search Strategy

*"Nothing is particularly hard if you divide it into small jobs."*
*–Henry Ford*

With your career plan in hand (and your life in balance), it's time to take action and land your ideal job. Sound easy enough? It can be, provided you approach it the right way. Consider the following two examples of people conducting a job search.

Vivian has worked in marketing for about five years and now is interested in becoming a manager. She starts looking for job vacancies that have been posted by private companies and other organizations with marketing departments. She consistently checks the classified ads. She registers with an employment agency, which tells her that her resume will be mailed out to prospective employers. In addition, she posts her resume with an electronic job search firm. With all these people working for her, Vivian figures her resume is just about everywhere and her next job is just around the corner. Her work is done.

Sue is also looking for a marketing manager position and shares the same skills and experience as Vivian. She decides to market her skills directly to prospective employers. She begins by identifying the hiring managers in organizations that interest her. She sends her cover letter and resume to these hiring officials and then follows up her mailing with a phone call asking for an interview. She develops her network–those people who can provide her with information that may lead to a job. She conducts informational interviews with marketing directors to learn more about the position she is interested in. She also goes to conferences to meet other professionals in the field. She never once looks at a classified ad or browses the Internet for jobs. She thinks Monster.com must be a Web site for horror movie fans.

Who is likely to have more success? Most people would put their money on Vivian (or at least take a similar approach), but in reality, Sue will probably be the first person to receive a job offer. All the research regarding the job search suggests that people find most jobs by accessing the hidden job market–those jobs that haven't even been posted yet–using the strategies that Sue does.

They don't call it the hidden job market for nothing, of course; finding these jobs requires some effort. That is why most people simply send out or post resumes and rely on search firms to do the work for them. Of course, those same people are still waiting on a company to find their resumes long after that same company has hired someone who went through the trouble of making direct contact. More often than not, Vivian's still waiting to hear back from the company that already hired Sue.

Of course, that doesn't mean you shouldn't post your resumes on the Internet or use job search services. You will probably find the best results by using a combination of approaches. Just remember that in today's economy, finding the job you want takes self-discipline, hard work, and self-motivation. A systematic and well-organized approach to finding a job is crucial. The trouble is, most people don't have one.

# How People Traditionally Find Jobs

Traditional approaches for finding employment involve contacting as many employers as possible with the hope that some of them will respond to you and set up an interview. This approach depends on the notion that the more classified ads you respond to, the more electronic resumes you post, and the more prospective employers who see your credentials, the more interviews you'll land. This is the "numbers game" job search. Traditional approaches also involve getting other "career experts" in employment services to help you find job leads and match you with available jobs. The traditional job search uses some or all of the following tools:

- **Job-training programs:** In most job-training programs, a job developer goes out and initiates employer contacts. After identifying potential openings, counselors screen individuals to determine an appropriate "match" between client and job. Clients are then referred to the employer for interviews.

- **Employment agencies:** In employment agencies, a "placement specialist," who has access and knowledge of particular job openings, will refer qualified individuals to prospective employers for a fee. Recruiters and headhunters typically use this process to find jobs for their clients. In these systems, the job seeker tends to be at the mercy of the agency, and a very limited number of the people who rely on this method find employment.

- **Job postings:** Employers with openings often post them to job banks. Job banks are systems of postings, including small systems, such as the newspaper "want ads," and large systems, such as Internet job posting sights (like Monster). Anyone can apply for posted job bank positions. The major drawback to this method is that you must compete with all the other job seekers who may be remotely qualified for the advertised positions.

- **Resumes:** Most job seekers spend hours searching through want ads from local newspapers and mailing hundreds of resumes to employers. They also "pound the pavement"–going from business to business to fill out applications and leave resumes with prospective employers. The problem with this approach is that you must rely on the strength of your qualifications on paper–resumes, cover letters, and employment applications–and don't get any face time with the person who can hire you.

The truth is, relatively few people find jobs with these approaches. Nontraditional job search approaches, on the other hand, are more proactive. Nontraditional approaches involve identifying prospective employers based on the development of a career plan, developing a network of contacts, and making direct contact with employers before jobs have even been posted.

# The Job Search Proficiency Scale

Because no single method of job hunting is 100 percent effective, you must be proficient in a variety of job search strategies. Moreover, you need to approach each phase of the job search with the right attitude and an action plan. The assessment that follows can help you gauge how effective your job search strategy is and then help you discover ways to enhance it.

For each activity statement below, choose the number of the response that best reflects how effective or skilled you are at the given task.

This is not a test. Since there are no right or wrong answers, do not spend too much time thinking about your responses. Be sure to respond to every statement.

| | Very Effective | Somewhat Effective | A Little Effective | Not at All Effective |
|---|---|---|---|---|
| **In looking for a job, how effective am I at...** | | | | |
| 1. posting my resume on Internet job boards | 4 | 3 | 2 | 1 |
| 2. identifying companies I would like to work for | 4 | 3 | 2 | 1 |
| 3. networking for job leads | 4 | 3 | 2 | 1 |
| 4. conducting informational interviews with prospective employers | 4 | 3 | 2 | 1 |
| 5. going to conferences where I can meet people in similar positions as me | 4 | 3 | 2 | 1 |
| 6. searching the "want ads" in local papers | 4 | 3 | 2 | 1 |
| 7. signing with a headhunter who can help me find a new position | 4 | 3 | 2 | 1 |

Section I Total: _____

| | Very Effective | Somewhat Effective | A Little Effective | Not at All Effective |
|---|---|---|---|---|
| **In presenting my qualifications in writing, how effective am I at...** | | | | |
| 8. writing an outstanding, professional resume | 4 | 3 | 2 | 1 |
| 9. writing a cover letter that grabs an employer's attention | 4 | 3 | 2 | 1 |
| 10. filling out applications correctly | 4 | 3 | 2 | 1 |
| 11. stating my job objective | 4 | 3 | 2 | 1 |
| 12. adapting my resume for electronic viewing | 4 | 3 | 2 | 1 |
| 13. obtaining references who have written letters on my behalf | 4 | 3 | 2 | 1 |
| 14. developing a portfolio of my best work | 4 | 3 | 2 | 1 |

Section II Total: _____

| | Very Effective | Somewhat Effective | A Little Effective | Not at All Effective |
|---|---|---|---|---|
| **In interviewing for jobs, how effective am I at...** | | | | |
| 15. researching the organization and industry ahead of time | 4 | 3 | 2 | 1 |
| 16. effectively answering interview questions with specific examples | 4 | 3 | 2 | 1 |
| 17. making a good first impression | 4 | 3 | 2 | 1 |
| 18. dressing and grooming for success | 4 | 3 | 2 | 1 |
| 19. highlighting my strengths and camouflaging my weaknesses | 4 | 3 | 2 | 1 |
| 20. preparing a list of questions to ask prospective interviewers | 4 | 3 | 2 | 1 |
| 21. staying upbeat and enthusiastic about the job | 4 | 3 | 2 | 1 |

Section III Total: _____

| | Very Effective | Somewhat Effective | A Little Effective | Not at All Effective |
|---|---|---|---|---|
| **When following up after interviews, how effective am I at...** | | | | |
| 29. sending thank-you notes and e-mails | 4 | 3 | 2 | 1 |
| 30. telephoning employers if I do not hear from them | 4 | 3 | 2 | 1 |
| 31. obtaining the business cards of interviewers | 4 | 3 | 2 | 1 |
| 32. keeping accurate records of all employers with whom I interview | 4 | 3 | 2 | 1 |
| 33. assessing job offers | 4 | 3 | 2 | 1 |
| 34. negotiating salary, benefits, and other compensation | 4 | 3 | 2 | 1 |
| 35. providing additional materials requested by prospective employers | 4 | 3 | 2 | 1 |
| **Section IV Total:** _____ | | | | |

## Scoring

This assessment can measure how competent you are in four critical aspects of the job search. Add up the scores you circled for each section. Put that number on the line marked "Total" at the end of each section, and then transfer your totals to the spaces below:

Section I: Using a Total Marketing Approach _____   Section III: Interviewing _____

Section II: Paper Job Search Methods _____   Section IV: Follow-up _____

# Improving Your Job Search Strategy

Not everyone has skills in every aspect of the job search. In fact, most of us have one or two weaknesses that we point to as the reason we don't gain an interview or an offer. Someone who can create a knockout resume may clam up at an interview. Likewise, someone who shines in the personal exchange of an interview may not have the slightest clue how to organize a job search.

Although you aren't expected to master every nuance of a job search strategy, the better you are at the four critical aspects listed above, the better your chances of getting the job you want. The key is to identify your weaknesses and take the necessary steps to improve them.

For each scale above, a score from 7—13 is low and suggests that you need to develop more job search competencies in this area. A score from 22—28 is high and suggests that you have a good handle on this aspect of the job search and should keep up the good work.

What follows are strategies for improving your job search strategy. As you read through the suggestions and complete the exercises, concentrate on those scales that you scored in the low or average ranges. And remember that all the planning and introspection you've done to help define your dreams won't get you far if you aren't prepared to take the necessary steps to fulfill them.

# *The Total Marketing Approach*

For many, the job market appears to be a maze that consists of dead ends, blind alleys, and endless frustrations. The typical "hit-or-miss" approach to finding a job often results in a lengthy job search, which, in turn, results in the job seeker taking the first thing that finally comes along, whether or not he or she wants it. The only way to effectively navigate the maze is to understand how employers fill job openings.

To better understand the job market, you need to understand the two basic types of jobs for which you will apply: the visible ones and the hidden ones.

Visible job leads are those vacancies that have been officially announced by an organization. Organizations traditionally make the general public aware of these openings by placing an ad in newspapers or magazines, having the personnel department announce it, retaining a search firm, making employment agencies and placement offices aware of it, and alerting state government agencies. At that point, you–and millions of other people–open a newspaper or a Web browser and see a job opening that interests you.

Although it appears easier to get a visible job, it's not often the case, primarily because of competition. Most job openings are actually never advertised, yet most people only apply for the visible jobs. Thus, you have a large percentage of job seekers squabbling over a small percentage of available jobs. Imagine a grocery store advertising a particular brand of soda on sale at the front of the store. Imagine 100 customers fighting over the 10 cases that the store has available in that front display. Now imagine that one guy in the soda aisle, far from the maddening crowd, who not only has several cases of the on-sale soda sitting right in front of him but a dozen other options besides. Applying for visible jobs is like fighting for one of those cases at the front of the store. Odds are good that you will come away empty handed or with something you don't really even want.

It is true, however, that millions of people do find jobs by searching the want ads, using employment agencies, or responding to Internet postings. So, even though it shouldn't command your undivided attention, trying to get a job in the visible market can still be a worthwhile endeavor. The following strategies can help you make the most of this approach:

- Use the employment clearinghouse functions of professional and trade associations to search for vacancies.

- Attend career fairs sponsored by colleges and chambers of commerce.

- Avoid personnel departments because they usually do not have the power to hire applicants, only to screen them out.

- Set up a place in your home to better organize your job search–a place where you can keep track of contacts, interviews, and follow-up opportunities.

Most people aren't aware of jobs on the hidden market because they have not been announced; in fact, there may not be an official job opening. The two primary methods for tapping the hidden job market are directly contacting employers and networking.

# Making Direct Contact

Nearly half of all people get their jobs by contacting employers directly, often through a direct mail campaign or a simple phone call. To enhance your chances of success, you should

1. **Research and screen organizations of interest:** Determine the most appropriate companies to contact by finding out the size and type of the organization, where they are located, and what products and services they provide.

2. **Identify hiring officials in these organizations:** Call the company to request this information. Get the exact spelling and proper title of the person who can hire you, usually the manager in the department you would work in.

3. **Develop a well-crafted cover letter and resume:** Send a resume and an individualized cover letter addressed to this hiring official.

4. **Develop a well-planned telecommunication presentation:** You should call three to four working days after your resume and cover letter have likely arrived. Be prepared for this phone call by writing out a script of what you want to say.

5. **Be sure to ask for an interview:** Even if there are no openings, ask to see this person to discuss the organization's goals and possibilities for future employment.

The following resources are useful for identifying potential organizations that fit with your career goals and could use your skills. Just don't forget all the work you've done so far, and look for opportunities with companies and organizations that will match your values, interests, and skills and fill your needs.

- **Chamber of Commerce:** This can be a good source for identifying organizations in your community. It publishes a list of companies in the area.

- **Library:** This is a great place to start researching prospective employers. Sources that are available in most libraries include the following:

  - Standard and Poor's *Register of Corporations, Directors, and Executives*

  - Trade journals such as *Dun's Review* and *Advertising Age*

  - Business periodicals such as *Forbes* and *Fortune*

  - *Encyclopedia of Associations*

  - Dun's *Employment Opportunities Directory*

  - *The Directory of Executive Recruiters*

  - Newspapers from cities where you might like to work

- **Yellow pages:** The yellow pages will help you discover local companies that may offer jobs in your selected career field. Contact these companies through networking, cover letter and resume submissions, and/or by telephone.

- **The Internet:** Nearly every organization you might want to work for has a Web site. Simply searching the name of the industry you'd like to work in along with the city you live in (or are willing to relocate to) will give you a ton of options and information.

## Networking

Although it may sound cliché, it is often "who you know" and not "what you know" that leads to a job. Networking is the process of systematically meeting people who can provide you with information that may result in an interview. You must learn to tap into your network–all the people you know who could help you–and milk them for those leads.

Networking serves several functions. It not only helps you access the hidden job market, but it also gets your name out there, letting people in the world of work know who you are, what you can do, and that you are interested in a job.

A network is made up of people you currently know and people you will soon meet. From the following exercise, you should generate an initial network of 25 to 50 people.

---

**EXERCISE**

### Identify your current network of contacts.

Contacts are people you already know, such as friends, relatives, family, people with whom you have worked, former teachers, and so on. List the people who could help you find a job in the space below:

_____

_____

_____

_____

### Identify contacts employed by prospective employers.

Identify several companies for whom you would like to work. Do your research to identify potential hiring officials with these companies. Then, list the name(s) of people who could provide you with a potential contact at each company you list:

Employer 1: _____

Employer 2: _____

Employer 3: _____

---

### INFORMATIONAL INTERVIEWING

Remember that the purpose of an informational interview is to gather information in order to confirm your career plans, become better known in your field, and expand your network of contacts.

If an employer you contact insists that there are no foreseeable job openings, an informational interview should be your next request. While not all employers will have the 30 minutes to spare, many will meet with you to discuss the industry, the organization, or the kind of job that might interest you.

---

## *The Paper Job Search*

Put frankly, a resume will seldom, if ever, land you a job. At best, it can land you an interview. Often, it is meant merely to screen you out. Still, the resume, like the other parts of the "paper job search," is a requirement–a ticket you have to have to even play the game. As such, you need to be proficient in using a variety of paper job search methods, from writing resumes and cover letters to filling out job applications and creating portfolios.

> **NOTE**
>
> A resume isn't intended to get you the job–it is intended only to get you an interview. Once there, you will have the chance to really sell yourself to the employer.

## The Resume

Resumes serve several purposes, for both you and prospective employers:

- **Self-assessment:** Developing and writing your resume forces you to determine your career objective, reflect on your past experiences, and assess your past accomplishments.

- **Generate interest:** Your resume will generate interest for prospective employers and prompt them to call you for an interview.

- **Make an impression:** Your resume will be an employer's first impression of you. In their review of your resume, employers will make assumptions about your organizational skills, your attention to detail, and your communication skills as well as evaluate your qualifications and past experience.

- **Provide information:** Your resume provides you with detailed information about your work experience, education, and skills. This information will be vital in other aspects of your job search.

- **Follow-up emphasis:** Leaving your resume with a prospective employer can help reinforce the positive impressions you made during an interview.

Of course, the most important function a resume serves is as a screening tool. Employers use resumes to weed out candidates they feel don't have the necessary skills and experience to do the job.

> **NOTE**
>
> You can often fill gaps in your work experience by listing volunteer work or self-employment.

> **N O T E**
>
> Use industry-specific keywords in describing your education and experience.

Because it is such an important job search tool, and one with its own rules and conventions, it is important that you concentrate on making your resume attractive, easy to read, informative, and, above all, professional. The following tips can get you started drafting your resume (or revising a current one):

- **Personal information:** This should include your name, present address (including ZIP code), telephone number (including area code), and an e-mail address.

- **Job objective:** Always include a specific statement that identifies the type of position you are applying for; for example, *Computer programming position with an emphasis in software development.*

- **Educational background:** You should list postsecondary schools you have attended (the most recent first), degrees received, major(s), minor(s), and dates of graduation. You may emphasize concentrations of coursework and other academic honors. If your overall grade-point average is 3.0 or better, include this information. Except in unusual circumstances, the name of your high school and dates of attendance are not necessary.

- **Work experience:** You must include a summary of your work experience, emphasizing the most recent or most important job relevant to your stated job objective. Include all types of work experience (full-time employment, volunteer experiences, summer employment, part-time employment, internships, and so on). List the title of your position, name of employer, dates of employment, and describe the nature of your work in detail. You should emphasize your strengths in this section of your resume.

- **Interests and activities:** Prospective employers are interested in your leisure activities (especially if they directly relate to your job objective). Identify any organizations to which you belong and any offices you hold in those organizations. Also, include any honors received, committees served on, workshops attended, and presentations given.

- **References:** State that letters of reference are "Available upon request." Then, be sure to select at least three individuals who are familiar with your qualifications and who are willing to write you a favorable letter. These references can be former employers, supervisors, coworkers, long-time acquaintances, or former teachers.

### PRESENTING YOURSELF WELL ON PAPER

Use the following tips to ensure a professional resume:

- Check your spelling, grammar, and punctuation. Then, have two or three other people double-check it. Misspellings and typographical errors suggest that you are sloppy and careless.

- Leave adequate margins on each side (one inch is typical).

- Single-space the text within the resume.

- Emphasize important aspects of your resume by using boldface type, uppercase letters, and underlining.

- Use "bullets" to highlight key accomplishments.

- Don't crowd too much information on your resume. Leave considerable "white space" so that your resume is easy to read.

- Print your resume on good-quality, heavy paper.

While these tips should be enough to get you started, this only covers the bare essentials of resume writing. You should consult other resources to create a more polished resume. Most resume books contain samples to inspire you, as well as in-depth advice on how to make your documents stand out from the crowd. Possible titles of interest include *Resume Magic* by Susan Britton Whitcomb and *Gallery of Best Resumes* by David Noble.

**N O T E**

Functional resumes that highlight skills and abilities rather than chronologically list and summarize education and work experiences can be effective for people with limited work experience or gaps in their work history.

## Cover Letters

You will want to include a cover letter with each resume you send to employers. Cover letters introduce your resume and highlight important aspects of your background. They also give you an opportunity to indicate why you are the best candidate for the job by directly matching your own qualifications with the job description. A well-written cover letter is one of the surest ways to ensure that a prospective employer reads your resume. Cover letters usually contain following parts:

- **Your address and the date**

- **Inside address of the organization**

- **Salutation:** Usually Dear Mr./Ms./Dr. and then the name of the person who is in a position to hire you. Always be sure to include a specific name; do not write "To Whom It May Concern." If you do not have this information, call the company and get it.

- **Introductory paragraph:** The introductory paragraph should immediately grab the reader's attention and compel him or her to read the rest of the letter. It should be individually tailored to the specific reader or prospective employer, should include the title of the position you are applying for, and should mention the names of any contacts that lead you to that position. (Remember, employers are more likely to hire people they know or at least people recommended to them by people they know.)

- **Middle paragraph:** This pivotal paragraph indicates why you are interested in the position, the company, its products or services, and, above all, what you can do for the employer and the value you can bring to the organization. Create interest by explaining how your unique qualities and characteristics make you a qualified candidate for the position, but try not to simply repeat the same information the reader will find in the resume.

- **Final paragraph:** In the closing paragraph, state your appreciation and indicate your desire for a personal interview. Include your phone number in the letter. Refer the reader to the enclosed resume. If possible, close your letter with a statement or question which will encourage a response or initiate follow-up plans. State that you will call in several days.

- **Closing:** Use a formal closing (such as "Sincerely"), and be sure to save room for your signature above your name.

Your cover letter demonstrates your professionalism as well as your ability to communicate effectively through writing. Keep your letter brief (one page if possible) and focused. Proofread it carefully to make sure it is free of misspellings and mistakes. Remember that a well-written cover letter, along with an effective resume, can help you get your foot in the door for an interview. Also, be aware that this represents only the most basic guidelines. For more in-depth information on how to write a cover letter, consult books at your local library. Possible titles of interest include *Cover Letter Magic* by Louise M. Kursmark and Wendy S. Enelow and *Gallery of Best Cover Letters* by David Noble.

## The Employment Application

The employment application may or may not be important in your job search. Some organizations don't bother with them until the interview process. Many others use it as the first point of contact, insisting that you fill one out before being considered for an interview. Regardless of when you fill one out, employment applications serve one basic function: to help organizations screen out unqualified applicants. Therefore, any applications you fill out must be as impressive and accurate as possible.

The following tips can help you fill out employment applications effectively:

- **Think before you write:** If at all possible, take the application home and complete it. This will give you more time to think about your answers before writing them down. Try to avoid cross-outs and erasures, since these give an employer a negative impression.

- **Use an ink pen:** Take several blue or black ink pens with you. Never use a pencil or a red or green ink pen.

- **Follow directions:** Read all instructions carefully before filling out an application. If there is something on the form that you do not understand, always ask the receptionist, personnel officer, or human resources assistant for clarification.

- **Neatness counts:** Print as neatly as possible. Your application is a reflection of you: If it is neat and accurate, then an employer can assume that you are neat and accurate.

- **Spelling is crucial:** Spell all words correctly. If possible, carry a pocket dictionary with you when you apply for a job.

- **Be honest:** Never lie on an application. If you provide false information to an employer, you can be fired and/or prosecuted for a criminal offense.

- **Attach a resume:** You can attach a resume to your application form, but never write "See Resume" on the application in lieu of answering all the questions. This suggests laziness on your part.

# *Interviewing*

When you hear the words "employment interview," what do you think of? Sweaty palms, pregnant pauses, and the feeling that you are being interrogated? It's a little disheartening to think about all the hard work you put into preparing your resume and cover letter, developing your network, and hunting for the ideal job, only to realize that someone will decide your entire career in a span of less than an hour. Even though this isn't true, it feels like it to most people.

The employment interview is at the heart of the job search process, and you must approach it without fear and apprehension. To do so, you must prepare as best as you can.

Proper preparation for an interview starts long before the interview itself. Individuals who are convinced they are the best candidate for a position will be most influential with the interviewer. Review your strengths and your accomplishments. If you're not convinced that you would be an asset to the employer's organization, the employer probably won't be either. Use the following strategies to help you prepare for and succeed at your interviews:

- **Analyze your strengths and weaknesses:** Start by doing some honest self-assessment (you should be good at it by this point). Analyze your strengths and weaknesses, your background, your academic performance, your vocational interests, and your personal aspirations and values. Formulate, in your own mind, not only what you would like to do but what you feel you are best prepared to do. Much of the work that you've already done in this book should help you.

- **Read employer literature:** Research your prospective employers. It is imperative that you have some knowledge about their policies, philosophies, products, and services. Some pertinent facts would be how old the organization's products or services are, what its growth has been, and how its prospects look for the future. This information provides topics for discussion during the interview. It is also quite helpful to try to identify how all this information relates to your interests and potential job duties. You can use the following strategies to uncover information about prospective employers:

  - Go to the library to read reference materials that contain information about the organization, including annual reports.

  - Read over material distributed by the organization's personnel or public relations office.

  - Visit the organization's Web site to learn as much as you can about its products, services, and history. Most companies have an "About Us" page that provides useful background information.

  - Talk with current employees of the company.

- A stockbroker could be useful in determining the stability of the organization, new product lines, and new marketing areas of publicly held companies.

- Contact distributors and/or competitors. Talk with employees of similar companies.

- **Prepare for commonly asked questions:** The questions an interviewer might ask during an interview will take many forms, but you can at least prepare for some of the most common ones.

---

### COMMON INTERVIEW QUESTIONS

- Why should I hire you?
- What qualifications do you have that will make you successful with our organization?
- What do you consider to be your greatest strengths?
- What do you consider to be your greatest weaknesses?
- In what ways do you think you can make a contribution to our company?
- What are your short- and long-term goals and objectives? How are you preparing yourself to achieve them?
- What do you see yourself doing X years from now?
- What do you expect to earn in X years?
- Why did you choose this career?
- How would you describe yourself?
- How do you think a friend or colleague who knows you well would describe you?
- What motivates you to put forth your greatest effort?
- How do you determine or evaluate success?
- What do you think it takes to be successful in a company like ours?
- What qualities should a successful manager possess?
- What two or three accomplishments have given you the most satisfaction? Why?
- What school subjects did you like best? Least?
- How do you work under pressure?
- What have you learned from your mistakes?
- Why did you decide to seek a position with this company?
- How do you feel about relocating?
- Are you willing to travel?
- Give me an example of a major problem you've encountered and how you dealt with it.

- **Prepare questions for the interviewer:** Interviewers expect you to ask questions and should give you a chance to do so. Not having any questions suggests a lack of interest in the job or the organization. You should develop a list of questions you would like to ask the interviewer beforehand. However, never ask a question that is easily answered in the materials supplied by the employer. As you research for the interview, jot down questions–similar to the ones listed below–that concern you.

---

### QUESTIONS TO ASK AN INTERVIEWER

- How much travel is expected?
- Can I progress at my own pace or is it structured?
- Will I spend most of my time working alone or with others?
- How frequently do you relocate professional employees?
- How much contact and exposure to management is there?
- Is it possible to move through the training program faster?
- About how many individuals go through your program each year?
- How much freedom is given and discipline required of new employees?
- How often are performance reviews conducted?
- Is it possible to transfer from one division to another?
- How much decision-making authority is given after one year?
- Have any new product lines been announced recently?
- At what time should I report for work?
- Does the organization provide employee discounts?
- Is a car provided to traveling personnel?
- What is the average age of top management?
- What is the corporate culture like?
- What are your policies on continuing education?
- What do you like best about working for this organization?

---

- **Plan your attire:** Because the first few seconds of the interview are critical in most hiring decisions, you will need to look your best. Dress professionally and also pay close attention to your grooming. While many companies have adopted an "office casual" work environment and dress code, it is better to be too conservative than too flashy.

- **Arrive early:** Try to arrive at least 10 to 15 minutes prior to the interview. Late arrival for a job interview is rarely excusable. Early arrival gives you a chance to review information about the organization and interviewer as well as your own skills and abilities.

It also gives you a chance to compose yourself. Just be sure to be courteous and professional with everyone you meet–anyone's opinion could factor into the hiring decision.

- **Greet the interviewer:** Always greet the interviewer by their last name, using Mr. or Ms. Never address the interviewer by a first name unless specifically instructed to do so. Always shake hands with the interviewer in a firm, confident manner. Stand until the interviewer asks you to sit.

- **Emphasize your strengths during the interview:** Emphasize your strong points with every answer you provide. The interview is your opportunity to sell yourself. Use "proof by example" to illustrate your skills. For example, instead of saying "I am an excellent salesperson," say "In my last position, I increased sales in my territory by 70 percent over 3 years."

- **Be enthusiastic:** Employers want to hire people who are excited about the work. You must project an air of confidence and enthusiasm about the interviewer's organization and the job you are applying for.

- **Close the interview professionally:** Always thank the interviewer for his or her time. Conclude by making a statement that sets the stage for appropriate follow-up activities, such as "I am very interested in working with your organization. May I call you next week to see if you need any additional information?"

**NOTE**

Never ask about salary during an interview–at least not until the offer is on the table.

Employment interviewing can be one of the most exciting experiences in your job search. The secret to your success is preparation and practice. Remember that the job does not always go to the most qualified person (although this helps); jobs often go to the candidate who is the best fit for the organization (personality, preparation, confidence, social skills, positive outlook on life, and enthusiasm). Therefore, you should view employment interviews as your chance to sell those qualities that make you an ideal employee.

# The Follow-Up

The feeling of relief that comes as you leave the building after an interview doesn't last long. The job search process doesn't end with a handshake and an "It was a pleasure meeting you." To cement the positive impression you've made, it is crucial to follow up.

## Giving Thanks

Follow-up letters or thank-you notes are an important and often-overlooked part of the job search. These are letters sent 24—48 hours after an interview or informational meeting. They are primarily intended to

- Reiterate your interest in the position.

- Thank the interviewer for the time he or she spent with you.

- Add pertinent information you may have overlooked in the interview.

- Keep the lines of communication open.

Of course, the content of the letter or note varies depending on the organization, the job in question, and the kind of interview it was. A note sent thanking someone for an informational interview will likely be shorter than one sent after a job interview. Still, in all cases, a thank-you note or letter should be short, professional, to the point, and free of errors.

You should begin writing your thank-you note immediately after an interview. The key is to reiterate your interest in the job and the organization while reminding the person you are writing as to what makes you a qualified applicant. The following example provides one possible approach to a thank-you note.

---

### SAMPLE THANK-YOU NOTE

Dear Ms. Smith:

Thank you for the time and courtesy you extended to me during our meeting on Wednesday. The position you described sounds extremely interesting and challenging.

I believe that my experiences as a secretary with the Private Industry Council and as an office manager with the Nationwide Insurance Agency would help me make a significant contribution to XYZ Corporation. I am very interested in helping your company grow and succeed.

If you need any further information or would like to meet again, please feel free to contact me at (606) 123-4567. I will contact you next week to discuss the next step in the selection process. Thank you again for your time.

Sincerely,

Nita Jobs

---

After each interview you complete, you should immediately send a thank-you note to all the people who interviewed you. Besides showing your appreciation and reiterating your strengths, thank-you notes also show that you have good attention to detail skills and good follow-through skills.

**NOTE**

You should also consider sending an e-mail immediately after interviewing and then follow that up with a mailed thank-you note.

## Assessing Job Offers

Part of the job search process is assessing the job itself once it has been offered. After all, what is the point of all this self-reflection and analysis–discovering your needs and interests, skills and values, goals and dreams–if you don't take the time to decide if a job is right for you?

Having been offered a job, your first instinct will be to immediately accept it. After all, rejecting it means going back to the job search. This is especially tempting if you have been unemployed for a long time. However, you should always examine each job offer very carefully. Items you should consider include:

- The company's financial position and financial history

- Promotional practices

- The type of work you will do

- The people with whom you will work

- The salary

- The benefits package

- The personality and management style of your supervisor

- Your commute to work

- Whether it will make the best use of your skills

- The amount of autonomy you will have on the job

- Opportunities for advancement

- How the job fits with your values

- How the job fills your needs

- How the job shifts your work-leisure balance

And don't lose sight of the forest while considering the trees. The temptation is to think of how a job offer will change your present—how it will solve your current problems, pay your bills, and provide you with the security you need. But it is also important to think about the long-term effects of your choices. How does this job change your overall career plan? Does it bring you closer to your long-term goals or is it just a paycheck? Does it open up new opportunities for you? Does it put you in contact with people who can help you make your dreams come true?

Take Sharon, for example. Sharon always wanted to own a beauty salon. She had eight years of experience working as a hairdresser at a chain store and had built up a base of loyal customers. Unfortunately, while she knew a lot about styling hair, she didn't know much about the numbers of running her own business. When a position opened up as an office assistant at a tax firm, Sharon saw it as an opportunity. Not only did the job pay more and offer better benefits, but it put her in contact with people who knew about money and taxes and what it would take to own her own business. Working at the tax firm for a few years might give Sharon the chance to save some capital, make some contacts, and learn the ins and outs of starting her own beauty salon.

So, as you consider a job offer, think back to everything you've discovered about yourself so far—your needs, your interests, your values, your career goals, and your career direction—and ask yourself if the offer represents just another job or the next step along your own career path.

## NEGOTIATING SALARY

A common misconception is that only executives can negotiate for their salary and other benefits. In reality, anyone can and should negotiate. Many employers are prepared to compromise if they want you bad enough and your requests are reasonable. The secret is to be assertive but not demanding in your discussions. Consider the following tips when entering salary negotiations:

- Let the interviewer initiate the discussion about salary. Once they throw out a number, you can negotiate.

- Come prepared by knowing the typical salary range for people working in similar positions. Research salary reference books in your local library or on the Internet.

- State your desired salary as a range. For example, if you know an employer wants to pay about $18,000/year, you might state your salary range as "upper teens to low twenties."

- Remember to negotiate other items in addition to salary.

- Ask for annual or biannual performance reviews to get possible salary increases based on your job performance. Many employers will negotiate for salary increases after a specified period of time.

- Show enthusiasm throughout the process.

Also, remember that money is not always the most important factor as you consider a job offer. Assess the overall package. Consider benefits such as flextime, vacation, job title, medical insurance, stock options, and so on. Also, consider often-overlooked benefits such as tuition reimbursement, assisted child care, or paid attendance to conferences and workshops.

# Tying It All Together

It is not enough to develop a career plan. You must now put that plan into action–more than likely by going out and getting the job you've dreamed of. Remember that finding a job is hard work and that you must use a combination of the visible and hidden job markets to get the one you want. If you learned more about your job search proficiencies and effective techniques for finding employment, you are now ready to go out and begin looking for your ideal job. The next chapter will help you learn to make better use of your specific personality style in searching for a job.

# CHAPTER 11

# Make the Most of Your Style

*"What lies behind us and what lies before us are tiny matters
compared to what lies within us."*
*–Ralph Waldo Emerson*

When I was growing up, my parents often wondered how my sister and I could be so different, despite being from the same genetic stock and raised in the same household. My sister liked predictability and took her obligations very seriously. I preferred new experiences and did not take anything seriously. She placed high value on home and family, whereas I often felt trapped by those types of commitments. My sister (like my wife) has a great work ethic, and I would rather not work at all. In short, my sister and I had–and continue to have–very different temperaments and approaches to life and career. The same is true for people searching for a job. For example, look at how differently four people go about looking for employment.

Janet likes to plan every little detail and stick to the tried-and-true job search methods. She is conscientious and willing to commit long hours to her job search. She uses a low-key approach to finding jobs, like sending out cover letters and resumes to employers she identifies through hours of Internet research, but she feels uncomfortable networking and interviewing.

Sherita is spontaneous, unstructured, and likes to use active job search methods. She has a high degree of energy and a great deal of enthusiasm. She does not like details and the paper-based aspects of a job search but prefers networking and "cold calling" to talk directly with prospective employers. The good rapport she develops with people serves her well in interviews.

Juan is goal oriented and determined in his search for a job. He is confident in his job-seeking abilities and direct in his approach, contacting employers and all but insisting on an interview. He is very good at networking and convincing prospective employers that he can improve their organization.

Eddie is easygoing and tends to rely on the visible job market, sending out resumes to advertised positions. He is not very good at making initial contact with employers, but he does well in interview situations with his relaxed and friendly style. He is not aggressive, but he is persistent in his low-key approach.

Which one of these approaches sounds most like you? You are undoubtedly a mix of styles, but you will probably find one approach that comes more naturally than others.

When it comes to looking for your ideal job, it is important to understand your temperament and its strengths and weaknesses. Once you better understand your temperament, you can better use the job search methods that come naturally to you as well as overcome your weaknesses by learning and incorporating more effective job search methods.

# Understanding Your Temperament

Your temperament is your unique way of expressing your feelings, thoughts, and actions. Temperaments are simple ways to understand yourself, your behaviors, and your relationships with other people. The study of temperaments has been useful in psychological practice, from marriage counseling to career counseling. In fact, a better understanding of your temperament can help you more effectively plan and execute your job search.

Temperament theory suggests that people of the same temperament type share a set of strengths, abilities, and core values. By becoming aware of these characteristics, you can better understand yourself and other people. Your temperament provides you with characteristics that set you apart from other people. The different combinations of these characteristics can lead to very different types of behaviors. An understanding of how your temperaments impact your behavior and the way you react to changes in your environment can even provide insight into your strengths and weaknesses as a job seeker.

## *The Four Temperaments*

The idea behind temperaments goes back to the days of togas and Trojans. Temperament theory comes from the work of the Greek doctor Hippocrates, who believed bodily fluids called "humors" caused certain human behaviors. These humors accounted for different behaviors in human beings. The key to healthy leaving, for Hippocrates, was to achieve the proper balance of these four humors. (If there was an imbalance, one cure was to drink enough poison to cause you to vomit, thus releasing the humor, or bodily fluid, you had in excess. This practice is not recommended.)

Of course, Hippocratic theories have evolved substantially over time, but the fundamental divisions have remained constant, as has the idea that these temperaments motivate our behaviors. Although many other systems have replicated or incorporated the temperament types proposed by Hippocrates, the four basic types remain consistent:

- **Sanguine:** Sanguine temperament types are generally optimistic, cheerful, confident, and popular. They can be impulsive and unpredictable. They tend to have a lot of energy but often have difficulty channeling this energy to accomplish the task at hand.

- **Choleric:** Choleric temperament types generally have a lot of ambition, energy, and drive. They often seem charismatic or dominating. They set lofty goals and work very hard to achieve them.

- **Melancholic:** Melancholic temperament types are generally thoughtful, analytical, and detail oriented. They tend to be perfectionists and are particular about what they want and how they want it. They are reserved and would rather work by themselves than as part of a group.

- **Phlegmatic:** Phlegmatic temperament types tend to be calm and unemotional. They are generally self-content, kind, relaxed, curious, and shy. They are reliable and compassionate toward others. They like routine and prefer to keep a low profile.

Hippocrates was the most famous physician of his time, and his writings about the four temperament types show their effect on people's physical health, mental attitude, happiness, career choices, and compatibility among people. However, it is important to remember that people cannot be categorized exclusively into one of four categories or labels. All people are some combination of these four temperament types. You will find that you possess one dominant temperament type, and the characteristics of that type will largely dictate your thoughts, feelings, and behaviors, but these types are used for better understanding people, not pigeonholing them.

## FACTS ABOUT TEMPERAMENTS

- You have a unique balance of the four basic temperaments.

- One of the temperaments will be dominant at your core.

- Whenever you're outside your "element," you'll probably experience discomfort.

- When exposed to people with a different temperament, you'll need to have time alone to find your proper balance.

- The more aware you are of how your temperament operates, the more empowered you'll be to develop solutions to problems.

- You can't change your basic temperament, but you can learn how to change behaviors and actions associated with that temperament if necessary.

# Temperament and the Job Search

Karen has a great eye for detail, a polished resume, and a well-organized job search plan, but she is uncomfortable contacting employers over the phone and meeting with them in person. She comes off as being quiet and reserved–it's just the kind of person she is. Karen soon discovered that she could "psych herself up" to talk with employers. If she worked at it, she could be outgoing and charismatic when interacting with new people; she could overcome a temperament quality that was inherent in her personality.

> **NOTE**
>
> An understanding of temperament can also help you better understand other people important in your job search. If you are able to understand the temperament of an interviewer, you can adapt to his or her temperament, such as keeping an interviewer who becomes easily distracted on topic by asking pointed questions.

Understanding your temperament can help you learn more about how you approach your search for employment and the reasons you choose certain job-seeking behaviors over others. Just as people who understand their personalities can better find jobs that will suit them, people who understand their temperament can maximize their strengths and take steps to overcome their weaknesses during the job search. Making small and reasonable accommodations will help you reduce the tension of a job search campaign and adjust to certain job search situations.

The following assessment can help you identify your type and learn how to integrate other types to be more effective in your search for the ideal job.

# The Job Search Style Inventory

The following assessment can help you identify your approach to career development and the job search based on your temperament. Read each statement to decide whether the statement describes you. For each choice listed, circle the number of your response on the line to the right of each statement.

This is not a test. Since there are no right or wrong answers, do not spend too much time thinking about your responses. Be sure to respond to every statement.

|   | Very Much Like Me | Usually Like Me | Occasionally Like Me | Somewhat Like Me | Not Like Me |
|---|---|---|---|---|---|
| 1. When in a group, I usually act as leader | 5 | 4 | 3 | 2 | 1 |
| 2. I am low-key and supportive | 5 | 4 | 3 | 2 | 1 |
| 3. I am a free spirit | 5 | 4 | 3 | 2 | 1 |
| 4. I am analytical | 5 | 4 | 3 | 2 | 1 |
| 5. I am a self-starter | 5 | 4 | 3 | 2 | 1 |
| 6. I do things in a leisurely manner | 5 | 4 | 3 | 2 | 1 |
| 7. I motivate others easily | 5 | 4 | 3 | 2 | 1 |

| | Very Much Like Me | Usually Like Me | Occasionally Like Me | Somewhat Like Me | Not Like Me |
|---|---|---|---|---|---|
| 8. I usually make rational, planned decisions | 5 | 4 | 3 | 2 | 1 |
| 9. I want to get ahead | 5 | 4 | 3 | 2 | 1 |
| 10. I am a good listener | 5 | 4 | 3 | 2 | 1 |
| 11. I enjoy making new things | 5 | 4 | 3 | 2 | 1 |
| 12. I am not very assertive | 5 | 4 | 3 | 2 | 1 |
| 13. Others look to me to make decisions | 5 | 4 | 3 | 2 | 1 |
| 14. I enjoy talking with other people | 5 | 4 | 3 | 2 | 1 |
| 15. I easily adapt to change | 5 | 4 | 3 | 2 | 1 |
| 16. I act only after having all the facts | 5 | 4 | 3 | 2 | 1 |
| 17. I am competitive | 5 | 4 | 3 | 2 | 1 |
| 18. I am loyal | 5 | 4 | 3 | 2 | 1 |
| 19. I do not like taking risks | 5 | 4 | 3 | 2 | 1 |
| 20. I pay close attention to details | 5 | 4 | 3 | 2 | 1 |
| 21. I tend to be task oriented | 5 | 4 | 3 | 2 | 1 |
| 22. I am patient | 5 | 4 | 3 | 2 | 1 |
| 23. I always have lots of energy | 5 | 4 | 3 | 2 | 1 |
| 24. I prefer to persuade people with logic | 5 | 4 | 3 | 2 | 1 |
| 25. I work hard to achieve my goals | 5 | 4 | 3 | 2 | 1 |
| 26. I am well organized | 5 | 4 | 3 | 2 | 1 |
| 27. I am good at juggling many tasks | 5 | 4 | 3 | 2 | 1 |
| 28. I prefer to work with facts and figures | 5 | 4 | 3 | 2 | 1 |
| 29. I am good at getting results | 5 | 4 | 3 | 2 | 1 |
| 30. I tend to develop only a few deep relationships | 5 | 4 | 3 | 2 | 1 |
| 31. I am innovative | 5 | 4 | 3 | 2 | 1 |
| 32. I like to make plans in advance | 5 | 4 | 3 | 2 | 1 |
| 33. I rarely take "no" for an answer | 5 | 4 | 3 | 2 | 1 |
| 34. I am caring and nurturing | 5 | 4 | 3 | 2 | 1 |
| 35. I see possibilities in every situation | 5 | 4 | 3 | 2 | 1 |
| 36. Others see me as inflexible and rigid | 5 | 4 | 3 | 2 | 1 |
| 37. I enjoy challenges | 5 | 4 | 3 | 2 | 1 |
| 38. I put people at ease | 5 | 4 | 3 | 2 | 1 |
| 39. I consider myself an "idea person" | 5 | 4 | 3 | 2 | 1 |
| 40. I prefer to work alone | 5 | 4 | 3 | 2 | 1 |

## Scoring

To score the assessment, first record your scores on the lines below. For example, if you circled "4" for item number 1, you would put a "4" in the first space.

Now add the totals for each column and then put that number on the total line at the bottom. You should get a total between 10 and 50.

| Scale I | Scale II | Scale III | Scale IV |
|---|---|---|---|
| 1 _____ | 2 _____ | 3 _____ | 4 _____ |
| 5 _____ | 6 _____ | 7 _____ | 8 _____ |
| 9 _____ | 10 _____ | 11 _____ | 12 _____ |
| 13 _____ | 14 _____ | 15 _____ | 16 _____ |
| 17 _____ | 18 _____ | 19 _____ | 20 _____ |
| 21 _____ | 22 _____ | 23 _____ | 24 _____ |
| 25 _____ | 26 _____ | 27 _____ | 28 _____ |
| 29 _____ | 30 _____ | 31 _____ | 32 _____ |
| 33 _____ | 34 _____ | 35 _____ | 36 _____ |
| 37 _____ | 38 _____ | 39 _____ | 40 _____ |
| **Total Doer** | **Total Preparer** | **Total Energizer** | **Total Thinker** |
| _____ | _____ | _____ | _____ |

# You've Got Style

How you go about the job search process largely depends on your job search style. Your job search style is your unique way of looking for employment based on your temperament.

Odds are, you have one score that is higher than the others. This represents your preferred job search style. Think of it as your default approach to a given job search situation–the one you are most comfortable with. It is important to recognize this preference for two reasons. First, it helps you discover your job search strengths–those aspects of the job search that come naturally to you. But it can also help you uncover possible weaknesses in your job search strategy. Not only does each style have weak spots, but styles that don't match your temperament (those you scored lower in) may offer positive strategies that you weren't aware of.

In other words, the key is to accentuate your strengths and improve your weaknesses–to identify those things you do in the job search that come natural to you but to also recognize the job search strategies that you struggle with and find ways

> **NOTE**
>
> A comprehensive job search requires you to use a variety of different tools and techniques in order to be successful. The problem that most people have when searching for their ideal job is that they use only a small number of the job search techniques available to them.

to overcome them, whether it's writing your resume, calling on employers, or answering interview questions. Once you recognize the role that your temperament plays in your job search strategy, you can learn to modify your behaviors to get the most from your job search.

The rest of this chapter provides descriptions of the four job search styles: their strengths, their weaknesses, and suggestions for making the most of them. As you read through the descriptions and complete the exercises, concentrate on the potential weaknesses of scales you scored higher in. Likewise, concentrate on the strengths of scales you scored lower on and find ways to incorporate the positives of those styles into your job search.

> **NOTE**
>
> No single job search style is better or worse than another. Although it's arguable that one or two styles are better suited to a particular aspect of the job search (that Doers are more naturally adept at interviewing than Thinkers, for example), the truth is that the job search is a complex array of tasks for which no single approach works all the time.

# *The Doer*

Doers are driven to achieve their goals. They are action oriented and assertive. They seldom take no for an answer and are highly competitive. They also have little patience and operate at a high stress level. Doers are self-motivated and results oriented, sticking with a task until it's finished. They take themselves very seriously. Because they are so forceful and intense, they often have trouble getting to know people well. They don't worry about details or offending other people. They are respected by others, however, because of their ability to get things done. They relate most closely to the Choleric temperament.

## Doers and the Job Search

Doers tend to be open and assertive with employers, whether over the phone or face to face. They excel at selling themselves to employers and following through on job search activities. Very articulate, they have no problem trumpeting their skills and experiences, but they tend to avoid criticism.

At the same time, Doers tend to lose patience with the job search. Their aggressiveness can be a liability, and they sometimes do not think about the consequences of their actions. They can come across as pushy, and they sometimes forget to (or choose not to) listen during a job search interview.

Not patient enough to rely on resumes and cover letters, Doers prefer job search strategies that get immediate results (such as directly calling an employer). Because of their aggressive and determined nature, Doers are also effective at building a job search network.

Fred is a Doer. He works as a journalist for a small-town newspaper, but he has a strong desire to get a better job. He drives himself more than his colleagues and sets both short- and long-term goals for his career and works hard to achieve them. He wants to find a job working for a bigger newspaper in a larger city and then become a managing editor. He believes that the secret to finding this job will be to meet directly with hiring officials at newspapers that could use his skills. When Fred meets with other newspaper executives in conferences, meetings, and trainings, he aggressively sells his qualifications and experience to prospective employers. He keeps business cards from all the people he meets while networking and keeps in touch with them through phone calls and e-mails. He has a resume (although it's a little unpolished) and a portfolio of the newspaper articles he has written but believes that networking with colleagues is the best way to get the job he wants.

Individuals with a primarily Doer style can improve their job search strategy with the following tips:

- Learn to know when assertiveness is detrimental to job search efforts.

- Think before acting.

- Learn to relax and be patient.

- Develop a portfolio of accomplishments to show employers.

- Do not alienate employers with a direct approach.

- Create a great resume and cover letter to show prospective employers.

# *The Preparer*

Preparers are good at interacting with others, provided they don't have to be forceful and can avoid conflict. They handle problems courteously and efficiently. They are well-organized and are adept planners. They find comfort in routine and prefer to keep a low profile. They carry out their well-designed plans in a thorough and persistent manner, although often without any outward show of enthusiasm. Preparers are very productive in their work. Their fear of change can become debilitating, but in a stable and predictable environment, they are friendly and warm and have a tremendous desire to succeed. They relate most closely to the Phlegmatic temperament.

## Preparers and the Job Search

Preparers remain calm in their search for a job, usually taking rejection in stride. Organized and thorough, they prepare for every aspect of the job search campaign, trying to anticipate all possible outcomes. Responsive listeners, their easygoing nature and affable personality make for a comfortable interview environment, although their sometimes shy nature may keep them from making a lasting impression.

Because they avoid confrontation and lack assertiveness, Preparers often struggle to sell themselves. They are not enthusiastic or aggressive when talking to employers, either to make initial contact or during job interviews. In an interview situation, especially, this temperament can come off as being passive–often seen as a negative in the world of work where companies are looking for energetic self-starters. Although nice guys don't finish last all the time in the job search, they often struggle to finish first.

A Preparer's easygoing temperament inclines them toward relying too heavily on the visible job market; thus, they are not very proactive in phoning employers, applying directly to organizations, or building a job search network. Being "people people," Preparers like to rely on others, such as friends, relatives, agencies or government offices, to help them in their job search–sometimes to the Preparer's detriment.

---

**PROFILE OF A PREPARER**

Janice is a Preparer. She is very friendly but somewhat shy when meeting new people. She works as a computer programmer in a student service office at a small college. She has worked at the college for 14 years and enjoys her job, but she wonders if she could get a job with a little more responsibility, such as an academic computing specialist who serves the entire college. She manages a well-organized job search campaign, especially with jobs advertised in the paper. She has developed a great resume and cover letter and sends it out if she sees a job she really likes, but she is not at all proactive in phoning potential employers or talking to people about potential openings they may have. If her dream job is never advertised, she will probably just stay in her current one.

---

Individuals with a primarily Preparer style can improve their job search strategy with the following tips:

- Take control of the job search campaign.

- Become more assertive in self-marketing.

- Learn to never take "no" for an answer.

- Be enthusiastic throughout the job search.

- Make an effort to achieve goals and not procrastinate.

- Take action after thorough preparation.

- Learn to enjoy talking with prospective employers.

- Build a network of potential employers.

## *The Energizer*

Energizers are adventurous and can be risk-takers. Spontaneous and unstructured, many people consider them to be "free spirits." Like Preparers, Energizers tend to avoid confrontation. Unlike Preparers, Energizers have a high energy level and a great deal of enthusiasm, although they often need help channeling their energy in constructive ways. Energizers get along well with almost everyone. They love a variety of tasks and are open to change. They can be impulsive and become restless easily. They would rather work with people than worry about details or paperwork. They may have limited organizational skills, which can lead to making careless mistakes, but their enthusiasm makes them good motivators. They relate most closely to the Sanguine temperament.

## Energizers and the Job Search

Energizers are willing to take risks. As such, they are willing to use all job search methods and will even discover innovative job search strategies. Energizers use their energy to propel them through every phase of the job search without getting discouraged. Their charisma and enthusiasm usually make a positive impression in an interview (provided they aren't seen as being hyper or chaotic).

Because their energy can be frenzied and they themselves are spontaneous, Energizers have difficulty organizing a job search campaign. They tend to be impulsive and careless. They are often not interested in the paper aspects of looking for a job (developing an effective resume, filling out employment applications, and so on), which can hurt their chances during the screening process. Although they can generate new ideas in their job search, they have difficulty developing a plan or following through to complete it.

Energizers are excellent at networking and talking directly with employers, although they sometimes have difficulty translating their energy and enthusiasm to paper. Thus, Energizers will excel in an interview, provided they haven't been screened out by a sloppy resume or a lack of attention to detail. Energizers also become bored easily in a job search campaign. They are okay as long as they are talking with people and networking. However, unless they are able to pull together all the aspects of a job search campaign, they will have difficulty finding the ideal job.

---

### PROFILE OF AN ENERGIZER

Shauna is an Energizer. She runs a small business from her home, selling paintings and other artworks, many of them her own. However, she does not make enough money at this and would like a job that would allow her to create art in her spare time. She worries that her personality might not come across well in interviews. She is also not interested in developing a resume, and would rather pay someone to do it for her. She is not at all organized and doesn't want to be bothered filling out employment applications. She says that she might create an electronic portfolio to show prospective employers her work. She might also send out "artsy" postcards to employers to advertise her skills. She feels that a creative approach to the job search will be the best way to sell her talents to prospective employers.

---

Individuals with a primarily Energizer style can improve their job search strategy with the following tips:

- Organize a job search campaign better.

- Learn to curb impulsiveness.

- Appreciate the value of tools such as resumes, cover letters, and employment applications (and working to make them professional).

- Learn not to be sensitive to criticism and rejection.

- Use creativity to find ways to impress employers.

- Attend more to the small details of an effective job search campaign (such as keeping track of resumes sent out, replies from prospective employers, interview dates, and follow-up activities).

# *The Thinker*

Thinkers are logical in all that they do–the Mr. Spocks of the job search style universe. Like Preparers, Thinkers are low keyed, although they prefer to work alone. They are not very assertive and often worry about things they can't control. Thinkers tend to be perfectionists, willing to spend a great deal of energy to complete projects and get them right. As a consequence, they often get bogged down in details and fail to "see the forest for the trees." Some would call them thoughtful; others would call them reclusive. They make decisions only after having all the facts. They have little tolerance for carelessness in themselves or in others, which prompts the impression that they are critical and impatient. They are most closely related to the Melancholic temperament.

## Thinkers and the Job Search

Thinkers need a lot of information before proceeding, whether that means researching a company before an interview or taking a battery of assessments to find out what careers they are suited for. They tend to operate a passive job search campaign, preferring more traditional methods–for example, mailing out a resume rather than directly calling an employer. Thinkers will work at finding a job for long hours and will not feel satisfied until they have completed the task at hand.

Their analytical nature makes them skilled at writing resumes and cover letters and preparing for job interviews, although once they come face to face with an employer, they may come off as being reserved and unenthusiastic. Thinkers are not very assertive in their search for employment and often struggle with networking. They may set unrealistic time limits for finding a job or get bogged down in the insignificant aspects of the job search and lose sight of the big picture.

Even the most organized job search won't produce results without risks. So, while a Thinker may feel prepared to take action, actually taking the action requires a little more effort on his or her part. Thinkers are adept at utilizing "paper" job search methods, such as sending out cover letters and resumes, completing employment applications, and following up after interviews.

> ### PROFILE OF A THINKER
>
> Omar is a Thinker. He tends to be extremely logical in his work as a geologist with the state of Virginia and would like to get a job as a geologist with one of the major U.S. oil companies. He likes the traditional job search methods, including mass mailing resumes and cover letters to all the oil companies he can identify through his research. He has posted his resume to all the job search engines, and he knows plenty about the companies he's most interested in. He is afraid to phone employers and talk to them directly, however, doubting his interpersonal skills. He knows that once he is on the job, he will do well, but he has trouble talking to prospective employers about his knowledge, skills, and abilities. He would be happy if an employer would just look at his immaculate resume and send him an e-mail telling him he's hired. He does very little networking and will simply wait for his resume to land in the right hands.

Individuals with a primarily Thinker style can improve their job search strategy with these tips:

- Rely less on logic and more on gut feelings.
- Don't fuss over the minor details of a job search campaign.
- Never lose sight of the big picture.
- Be less critical.
- Be flexible.
- Be more aggressive with employers.
- Develop a network of prospective employers.

# Improving Your Job Search Skills

We each have one or two styles that we will naturally gravitate toward. But remember that no one style is better than another. The best job search strategy is one that incorporates the best parts of your strongest style along with strategies you can learn to implement from weaker styles. While it is important to play to your strengths and stay in your comfort zone, odds are you won't fully realize your career goals without taking risks. Sometimes, that involves going against your natural inclinations and doing things you aren't comfortable with (such as picking up the phone and calling an employer) or don't think you're good at (such as networking or writing a cover letter). The more you engage in these activities, the better you will become at them. While temperament is a part of your personality, job searching is a skill that can be learned and improved. The key is to use your understanding of the one to help you improve the other.

In the spaces below, answer each question related to your job search style and ways it can be improved.

---

**EXERCISE**

What is your most dominant job search style?

_____

What are your job search strengths? Which job search strategies do you prefer to use?

_____

_____

What are your job search weaknesses? Which job search strategies do you least like to use?

_____

_____

What are some characteristics from other job search styles that you'd like to incorporate?

_____

_____

What steps can you take now to improve the effectiveness of your job search?

_____

_____

---

# Tying It All Together

The more you know about yourself and your tendencies, the better you are able to utilize the job search techniques that come naturally for your temperament as well as learn techniques that do not come naturally.

Having assessed your job search knowledge and learned about your job search style, almost nothing stands between you and your career goals. The final step is to ensure your success as you meet those goals. The last chapter will help you do just that.

CHAPTER 12

# Ensure Your Success

*"Many of life's failures are people who did not realize how close*
*they were to success when they gave up."*
*–Thomas Edison*

So, you've landed your ideal job. (And if you haven't, what's stopping you?) You may think your work is done, but in many ways, you're just getting started. Career development, after all, is about much more than getting a job offer. It's about managing the opportunities that come your way and working hard to create new opportunities of your own. You've spent most of this book setting long-term career goals; you want to be sure you reach them. That means ensuring you have the skills employers want most, regardless of what kind of job you've got.

Maintaining your career success means excelling at the work you do. This may be harder than you think. Just imagine working with (or managing) the following two employees.

Sam is a loner. He worries that if he asks for help, he will lose status in his supervisor's eyes. He is a poor team player and does not willingly share information with coworkers. He isn't receptive to others' ideas and is certainly not open to constructive criticism. He doesn't make much room for empathy or try to understand where his coworkers, or even his customers, are coming from.

Sherry appreciates being part of a team. She listens attentively to her coworkers and tries to learn as much as she can from them. She avoids passing judgment and trusts other people to accomplish the goals they set. She accepts both the strengths and weaknesses of the people in her office.

Although these two examples are exaggerated, they represent two of the many types of people you will encounter (or already have encountered) in the workplace. They each exhibit varying degrees of emotional intelligence (EI). Your emotional intelligence plays an important role in maintaining your career success.

# The Skills Needed to Succeed

In today's constantly changing world of work, people must take full responsibility for their own careers. In the 1950s and 1960s, workers could depend on loyal and consistent employment. Today, traditional career ladders have disappeared or been replaced, and employees who survive and succeed in the workplace are those who have a comprehensive set of skills–both the technical skills needed to do a job and the nontechnical or "soft" skills needed to be a good employee and team player.

Many researchers even suggest that these "soft" skills are more valuable than the technical requirements for a job. Employers are more concerned about workers showing up on time, taking supervision well, and getting along with each other than they are a worker's ability to complete a spreadsheet, track a package, or repair an engine. These "soft" skills can be loosely defined as emotional intelligence skills, and they are your keys to long-lasting career success. Emotional intelligence often determines not only who is hired, but also how successful an employee is with an organization.

Today's career managers (and that is what you are) must have a much wider array of emotional intelligence skills and knowledge to stay successful. Despite this fact, all the current research suggests that prospective employees do not have the emotional intelligence skills required to deal with the opportunities and challenges inherent in the world of work.

---

### WHAT EMPLOYERS WANT MOST

Employers worry about the gaps in skills in prospective employees. The National Association of Colleges & Employers (NACE) recently surveyed 640 randomly selected college recruiters in an effort to identify the most important performance dimensions currently being sought by employers in their prospective employees. In this study, the employers rated interpersonal skills as the most important skill for new employees to have, followed by ethics and integrity, leadership, perseverance, and then job-related knowledge. The first four most-sought-after dimensions were emotional intelligence skills.

---

## *Why Emotional Intelligence Matters*

The people with the highest emotional intelligence tend to be the ones who move ahead in their careers. The effectiveness of emotional intelligence training is well documented. In his book *Emotional Intelligence: Why It Can Matter More Than IQ*, Daniel Goleman suggests that people with well-developed emotional skills are more likely to be content and effective in their lives. Evidence verifies that people who are emotionally intelligent–those who know and manage their own feelings well and who read and deal effectively with other people's feelings–are at an advantage in any domain of life, from intimate relationships to business organizations. Knowing your best emotional intelligence skills and making the constant effort to improve them can help you to achieve the long-term career goals you've set for yourself.

Goleman identified a set of five emotional intelligence competencies:

> **NOTE**
>
> Unlike the traditional intelligence quotient (IQ), anyone can learn and improve his or her emotional intelligence skills. Emotional intelligence includes such skills as motivating oneself, thinking rationally, and empathizing with others.

I.   **Self-awareness:** Knowing one's internal states, preferences, resources, and intuitions

II.  **Self-regulation:** Managing one's internal states, impulses, and resources

III. **Motivation:** Emotional tendencies that guide or facilitate reaching goals

IV.  **Empathy:** Awareness of others' feelings, needs, and concerns

V.   **Social skills:** Adeptness at inducing desirable responses in others

Regardless of the type of organization you work for, you are evaluated on these skills. Your emotions can provide you with valuable information about yourself, other people, and interpersonal situations you will encounter in the workplace. Being successful means working together with coworkers and supervisors to meet the organization's goals. Ultimately, your emotional intelligence skills are teamwork skills.

You can increase your emotional intelligence by learning more about yourself and practicing these skills and abilities. But first, it might help to know what your stronger (and weaker) emotional intelligence skills are.

# The Emotional Intelligence Scale

The Emotional Intelligence Scale can help you determine how effective you are at working with others and what skills you could further develop to be more successful in your career. Read each statement to decide how well the statement describes you and then circle the number of your response on the line to the right of each statement.

There are no right or wrong answers, so do not spend too much time thinking about your responses. Be sure to respond to every statement.

| | Very Much Like Me | Somewhat Like Me | A Little Like Me | Not Like Me |
|---|---|---|---|---|
| 1.  I welcome constructive criticism | 4 | 3 | 2 | 1 |
| 2.  I attend all meetings on time | 4 | 3 | 2 | 1 |
| 3.  I am willing to help other coworkers | 4 | 3 | 2 | 1 |
| 4.  I appreciate differences in others | 4 | 3 | 2 | 1 |
| 5.  I communicate my ideas clearly | 4 | 3 | 2 | 1 |
| 6.  I am prepared to make sacrifices to reach goals | 4 | 3 | 2 | 1 |
| 7.  I foster team spirit | 4 | 3 | 2 | 1 |
| 8.  I acknowledge others' viewpoints | 4 | 3 | 2 | 1 |
| 9.  I communicate in a nonjudgmental manner | 4 | 3 | 2 | 1 |
| 10.  I keep the commitments I make to coworkers and supervisors | 4 | 3 | 2 | 1 |
| 11.  I acknowledge and reward coworkers for their contributions | 4 | 3 | 2 | 1 |
| 12.  I encourage differing opinions | 4 | 3 | 2 | 1 |
| 13.  I disagree with others tactfully | 4 | 3 | 2 | 1 |
| 14.  I make organizational goals a priority | 4 | 3 | 2 | 1 |
| 15.  I openly share new information with coworkers | 4 | 3 | 2 | 1 |
| 16.  I recognize the positive ideas of others | 4 | 3 | 2 | 1 |
| 17.  I ask questions and encourage others to do so | 4 | 3 | 2 | 1 |
| 18.  I maintain ethical standards when completing tasks | 4 | 3 | 2 | 1 |
| 19.  I trust other coworkers to complete their work | 4 | 3 | 2 | 1 |
| 20.  I empathize with others easily | 4 | 3 | 2 | 1 |
| 21.  I give others constructive feedback | 4 | 3 | 2 | 1 |
| 22.  I identify and respond to needs without being asked | 4 | 3 | 2 | 1 |
| 23.  I foster cooperation among coworkers | 4 | 3 | 2 | 1 |
| 24.  I am willing to change my mind | 4 | 3 | 2 | 1 |
| 25.  I listen attentively to others | 4 | 3 | 2 | 1 |
| 26.  I follow the rules and regulations of the organization | 4 | 3 | 2 | 1 |
| 27.  I encourage participation among uncommitted coworkers | 4 | 3 | 2 | 1 |
| 28.  I enjoy working with people different from me | 4 | 3 | 2 | 1 |
| 29.  I notice nonverbal and verbal cues | 4 | 3 | 2 | 1 |
| 30.  I complete tasks efficiently | 4 | 3 | 2 | 1 |
| 31.  I am cooperative | 4 | 3 | 2 | 1 |

| | Very Much Like Me | Somewhat Like Me | A Little Like Me | Not Like Me |
|---|---|---|---|---|
| 32. I respect the personal boundaries of others | 4 | 3 | 2 | 1 |
| 33. I learn as much as possible from my coworkers | 4 | 3 | 2 | 1 |
| 34. I hold myself accountable for my actions | 4 | 3 | 2 | 1 |
| 35. I coordinate my work with that of my coworkers | 4 | 3 | 2 | 1 |
| 36. I make the best use of everyone's strengths | 4 | 3 | 2 | 1 |

# Scoring

To score the assessment, first record each score on the lines below. For example, if you circled "4" for item number 1, you would put a "4" in the first space.

Now add the totals for each column and put that number on the total line at the bottom. You should get a total between 9 and 36.

| Scale I | Scale II | Scale III | Scale IV |
|---|---|---|---|
| 1 _____ | 2 _____ | 3 _____ | 4 _____ |
| 5 _____ | 6 _____ | 7 _____ | 8 _____ |
| 9 _____ | 10 _____ | 11 _____ | 12 _____ |
| 13 _____ | 14 _____ | 15 _____ | 16 _____ |
| 17 _____ | 18 _____ | 19 _____ | 20 _____ |
| 21 _____ | 22 _____ | 23 _____ | 24 _____ |
| 25 _____ | 26 _____ | 27 _____ | 28 _____ |
| 29 _____ | 30 _____ | 31 _____ | 32 _____ |
| 33 _____ | 34 _____ | 35 _____ | 36 _____ |
| **Total Communication** | **Total Commitment** | **Total Cooperation** | **Total Connection** |
| _____ | _____ | _____ | _____ |

# The Four Cs of Success

The Emotional Intelligence Scale can help you identify your strengths as an employee (or a supervisor) in four critical skills areas: communication, commitment, cooperation, and connection. The following sections will describe these four key components as well as provide some questions to help you enhance your emotional intelligence skills.

While anyone can benefit from the information and exercises that follow regardless of their score, you should concentrate on

**NOTE**

All employers want employees who are good team players, who communicate well, who collaborate with coworkers, and who can leverage diversity. At least, you'd be hard pressed to find an employer who doesn't appreciate these skills.

those areas you scored the lowest in. For each section, scores from 9—17 are considered low and suggest room for improvement, while scores from 28—36 are high and suggest this is one of your strengths. Naturally, you will want to play to your best skills to maintain your career success, but you shouldn't neglect any opportunity to turn a weak point into a strong one.

# *Communication*

Emotional intelligence is a critical component for success or failure in the world of work, and much of emotional intelligence relates to effectively sending and receiving messages. People with high scores in communication get their point across effectively but also listen attentively to what other people say. They communicate ideas in a clear and nonjudgmental manner, using both verbal and nonverbal cues. They are not afraid to ask questions or ask for help. They show a great deal of empathy and are good at resolving conflicts.

Miscommunication is the cause of much disagreement, both in and out of work. To be more effective in communicating with others, remember these key points:

- When sending messages, use words like "I," "me," and "my." In this way, you take ownership of your messages. Words like "They" or "Some people" are ineffective and elusive. Speak for yourself!

- Look at the person and speak to him or her directly. Maintain steady eye contact (but don't give them the "stare of impending doom").

- Express your feelings. It may sound cheesy, but your emotions drive your behavior and thus explain your actions and reactions. It can be useful to get them out in the open. Examples of how to express your feelings include statements such as "I get upset when you break your word."

- Give constructive feedback. Be generous in the amount and type of feedback that you give to others. Expressing more positive feedback can increase the quality of your working relationships.

- Be assertive. Assertive people can express their desires, needs, and wants. By establishing what it is that you really want, you will know what is worth fighting for and what to simply walk away from.

## Learn to Listen

Listening is paying close attention to what others say and is just as important as, if not more important than, sending your own messages. Active listening involves listening and responding to another person in ways that help you better understand his or her views. Too often, however, people find it much easier to talk than to listen. Here are some common blocks to effective listening:

- **Inadequate listening:** It is easy to get distracted from what other people are saying. This includes being too involved with your own thoughts or too preoccupied with your own needs.

- **Evaluative listening:** Listening with the intent of judging the person can hinder your ability to really understand them.

- **Daydreaming:** Everyone's attention will wander from time to time. If you find yourself having a hard time listening to someone, it is probably a sign that you are avoiding the person or certain topics of conversation.

- **Rehearsing:** Any time you ask yourself the question, "How should I respond to what the person is saying?" you get distracted from what the person says.

Active listening is a learned skill and one you can easily improve by following a few simple steps:

- **Listen for understanding:** Rather than think about what you will to say next, make it your priority to discover what other people are thinking and feeling as they relay their messages to you.

- **Clear your mind:** Be receptive to the thoughts and emotions behind other people's words. Use "encouragers" such as "Tell me more," "Uh, huh," or "I see."

- **Be like a mirror:** Reflect back to the person your understanding of his or her thoughts and feelings. In your own words, restate what you understand the person's message to be.

- **Ask for more:** Invite the speaker to elaborate if you need more information.

---

### I SEE WHAT YOU'RE SAYING

People frequently communicate without words (as most irritated drivers know) by using body action, eye contact, hand gestures, and facial expressions.

Here are some tips for enhancing your nonverbal communication skills. Remember that people from different cultures may show some variations on these tips:

- Find comfortable spacing when talking to another person. How close you get will depend on your relationship with the other person.

- Lean your body forward slightly. This will show the other person that you are interested in the conversation.

- Maintain eye contact.

- Provide nonverbal cues to the other person; for example, nodding your head in approval.

- Keep gestures simple and unobtrusive.

- Stay alert when communicating with others. Closing your eyes, yawning, or looking at your watch can block effective communication (a scientific way of saying "tick people off").

---

Answering the following questions can give you some insight into your strengths and weaknesses as a communicator. Remember that you can improve your communication skills, just as you can any emotional intelligence skill.

---

**EXERCISE**

When do you find yourself being so distracted that you do not listen to others?

_____

_____

_____

When do you find yourself thinking about your response instead of listening to others when they speak?

_____

_____

_____

How can you improve your communication skills?

_____

_____

_____

---

**NOTE**

For employees to feel committed, they must feel trusted, included, and supported. Trust your coworkers to do their jobs effectively and efficiently, support them in their work, and include them in your own, and they will return the favor.

# *Commitment*

People with high scores in commitment tend to be steadfast in their pursuit of organizational goals and dedicated to the success of their team. They show up prepared to work and are intuitive about what needs to be done. They complete the tasks that they are assigned and are accountable for the results.

Commitment to a team of coworkers and an organization can take many forms. Contrary to popular opinion, this does not include spending long hours at work or taking work home, refusing to take earned vacations, or obsessing about the work you do. Being committed is not the same as being a workaholic or a perfectionist.

Instead, commitment includes things such as

- Making personal sacrifices to meet a larger organizational goal.

- Finding a sense of purpose in your organization's larger mission.

- Using the organization's core values when you make decisions.

- Seeking out opportunities to further the organization's goals.

## Taking Responsibility

Personal responsibility refers to accepting the consequences of your actions, choosing the behaviors necessary to reach your goals, and making decisions that will positively affect the organization you work for.

When you accept responsibility, you make an effective, growth-oriented decision to create the future you want. You should begin to think about the projects that you might accept that will enhance your career development.

When you accept responsibility, you also choose to do the most important tasks on your agenda. If you find yourself avoiding hard projects out of fear or intimidation, you will want to reverse your self-defeating thinking or find a mentor to talk to about your fears.

> ── **N O T E** ──
>
> To be more responsible in the workplace, you need to be aware of your strengths. Think about your most valuable contribution to the organization— the thing that distinguishes you from your coworkers. The most successful people take on assignments that match their strengths.

### INCREASING YOUR PRODUCTIVITY

Being responsible includes improving your own productivity. Whether it's a teacher raising the test scores of more students, the lawyer winning more cases, or the sales manager exceeding a quota, every organization has a "bottom line" of some kind and will appreciate the employees who meet or exceed their goals.

Here are some habits and activities employees often engage in that decrease their productivity at work. Place a check mark in front of any you spend too much time doing:

- Spending too much time on e-mail
- Surfing (the Web, not the ocean, although most people shouldn't do that while at work either)
- Chatting excessively with coworkers
- Searching for misplaced paperwork
- Poorly prioritizing tasks
- Good, old-fashioned procrastinating
- Poorly estimating how long tasks will take
- Becoming obsessed with the details

Answering the following questions can give you some insight into your strengths and weaknesses in terms of commitment.

---

What commitments can you make to your organization?

_____

_____

_____

What situations in your life may affect your commitment?

_____

_____

_____

What can you do now to improve your level of commitment?

_____

_____

_____

---

# Cooperation

People with high scores in cooperation willingly help team members achieve organizational goals. They do whatever they can to enhance team spirit and acknowledge the accomplishments of their coworkers. They work to get everyone involved, fostering participation from committed and uncommitted team members alike.

Quite simply, cooperation represents your efforts to work with others. This does not include doing other people's work for them (even if you think you would do it better), giving in to others' suggestions all the time, or trying to avoid conflict. Giving in, giving up, or doing all the work yourself only isolates you further from people who can help you be successful. It also tends to foster negative feelings in the workplace.

Instead, you should find ways to develop effective working relationships with your coworkers, striving to create an atmosphere of camaraderie with clear lines of communication. This includes

- Sharing important information and resources with your team members. Sharing information builds trust and integrity, and sharing with your coworkers helps ensure that they will return the favor.

- Promoting a friendly and cooperative climate in which to work. Keep your criticism constructive, and remember to praise the good work of team members.

- Identifying and nurturing opportunities for cooperation. Learn to pick up on cues about projects that are important to coworkers and then collaborate with them.

## Giving Feedback

Positive feedback prompts your coworkers to continue doing things that benefit the organization. When giving positive feedback, consider the following tactics:

- **Be sincere:** Tell what you think of group members' behavior and how it had a positive impact on the outcome.

- **Point out the details:** Mention specific behaviors, actions, and events that were especially effective.

- **Make it personal:** Use "I" statements when possible. For example, you might say something like "I really enjoyed your marketing presentation. It really got me thinking. Keep up the great work."

> **NOTE**
>
> The first year in a new job is critical. New employees need to understand the corporate culture, learn the written and unwritten rules of the organization, and work to become an efficient member of the team.

## Providing Constructive Criticism

Constructive criticism provides information so that coworkers can improve their behavior. In providing constructive criticism, remember the following:

- Word your feedback so that it does not hurt or offend the person. Very few people appreciate having their shortcomings pointed out to them, so be very careful with the language you use.

- Identify specific behaviors and situations that need improvement. Try to balance these with praise of behaviors that you find effective.

- Tell how you feel about the behaviors and the outcomes rather than pass judgment on the individual's personal qualities.

- Confirm understanding by listening to the person's reaction.

- Most importantly, offer suggestions on how to improve performance. "Do it faster, better, cheaper" might be the ultimate goal, but give specific strategies for how to meet those goals.

### It's a Matter of Trust

To develop and maintain effective relationships with coworkers and supervisors, you must work to establish trust. A high level of trust is hard to build and may take years to develop. So, take your time in building trust with people, and don't expect coworkers to immediately trust you 100 percent either. Here are some things you can do to enhance trust in the workplace:

- Communicate accurate and relevant information.

- Openly share your thoughts and feelings with others.

- Be friendly (even if it's just not your day).

*(continued)*

*(continued)*

- Behave ethically in your relationships with others.
- Do what you say you will do.
- Avoid stereotyping.
- Build relationships with people from cultures and backgrounds different from yours.
- Support coworkers who are "on the spot."
- Be honest with coworkers and supervisors.

Answering the following questions can help you pinpoint ways to improve your cooperation skills. Remember that while people are often hired for their skills, they are often fired for their inability to get along with their coworkers or supervisors. Technical skills may be your ticket into a job, but your emotional intelligence skills are your ticket to long-term success.

---

### EXERCISE

When have you struggled to work as part of a team? What kept the team from functioning as effectively as it could have?

_____

_____

_____

What can you do to establish a more collaborative environment at work?

_____

_____

_____

What can you do to ensure that team members openly share ideas?

_____

_____

_____

---

## Connection

People with high scores in connection enjoy working with other people with diverse backgrounds. They feel connected to the other members of the team because they can see all the possibilities that those team members bring to the table. They are open to different points of view and encourage other team members to express their opinions. By recognizing and accepting the strengths and weaknesses of coworkers, people with good connection skills tend to operate from a more optimistic viewpoint.

When you cannot connect with coworkers and supervisors, you fail to create a cooperative, energetic environment that encourages all people to do well. Your ability to connect with others also significantly boosts your value to your employer.

To connect with other people in your organization, you need to be someone your coworkers appreciate and like to work with. In connecting with others, you should try to

- Be accessible, approachable, and responsive.

- Be adaptable in your work. Be creative and flexible during "crunch time," and be willing to accommodate other people.

- Maintain an upbeat, can-do approach in your work. Moodiness can lessen your connection to other people; try to maintain an even emotional keel.

- Be respectful and considerate of others—the time they give to you and the skills, knowledge, and abilities they bring to the organization.

- Be fair. You should always try to look for "win-win" solutions in every situation and avoid conflicts if possible.

## Being Empathetic

Empathetic people are uniquely attuned to the feelings of others. They can easily understand what people are going through. As such, they are also highly attuned to the messages hidden behind what people say. They are highly socially intelligent, tend to have very effective interpersonal relationships, and are guided by genuine feelings of compassion and regard for their fellow human beings.

Being empathetic involves several key skills, including

- Listening carefully to others' points of view.

- Setting aside your own judgments and biases in order to "walk in the shoes" of your coworkers.

- Paying close attention to both the verbal and nonverbal messages others send you.

- Drawing as much as possible on your own experience to relate to the circumstances of others.

## Leveraging Diversity

We live in a complex society, and interacting effectively with people from different cultures, ethnic groups, socioeconomic classes, races, and historical backgrounds is critical. The problem is that interacting with people different from us does not come naturally. The process of leveraging diversity is important because you will be required to interact with people despite natural barriers of culture, religion, work ethic, gender, race, and social class. In addition, you will inevitably encounter greater diversity among your friends, teachers, classmates, coworkers, neighbors, and others in your community. Therefore, you must be skilled in relating to diverse individuals.

Use the following worksheets to recognize and better understand the diversity of the people around you.

---

**EXERCISE**

Coworkers and friends who are different from me: _____

_____

How these friends are different (race, social status, religion, gender, culture, etc.): _____

_____

Reasons to appreciate those differences: _____

_____

---

**EXERCISE**

### Recognizing Strengths and Weaknesses

We all have a unique set of skills, abilities, talents, and traits that we bring to the workplace. Recognizing the strengths of coworkers and learning to bring out the best in them are important, whether you are a member of the team, a supervisor, or the owner of the company.

In the space below, list the members of your team (your coworkers) and any positive characteristics they have that can help the team and the organization reach their goals:

| Team Member | Positive Characteristics |
|---|---|
| _____ | _____ |
| _____ | _____ |
| _____ | _____ |
| _____ | _____ |
| _____ | _____ |
| _____ | _____ |
| _____ | _____ |

Answering the following questions can help you to imagine ways to foster a better sense of connection at work.

---

How can you use the differences of your team to be more effective at work?

_____

_____

_____

What can I do to be more open to the differences of the people around me (both in and out of work)?

_____

_____

_____

What can I do to be more empathetic toward the people around me?

_____

_____

_____

---

# Leading the Way

Being an effective part of a team in the workplace takes practice, experience, and persistence. Much of how you act as part of a team comes from other teams you have been a part of. One of the first steps to becoming successful is to explore your teamwork experiences in the past. This will give you insights into the strengths and weaknesses you possess in working with others. The following exercises can help you reflect on your team experiences in the past and how you might improve your ability to work as part of a team in the future.

Describe some of the teams on which you have worked in the past.

_____

_____

_____

Were they successful? Why or why not?

_____

_____

_____

What roles did you play on these teams?

_____

_____

_____

What team skills do you possess?

_____

_____

_____

What team skills do you need to develop further?

_____

_____

_____

What steps will you take to improve these skills?

_____

_____

_____

# Tying It All Together

During the course of your career, you will make extensive use of your emotional intelligence skills. You may find yourself speaking to angry clients or customers, listening to an anxious or frustrated supervisor, or getting into a disagreement with a coworker. The secret to success in today's workplace is to communicate effectively with your coworkers, commit to the success of your organization, cooperate to ensure that everyone's career goals are met, and find ways to connect emotionally with the people you work for and with.

Emotional intelligence skills are job skills you can learn. You don't have to be the smartest or best-educated person in your organization. You simply need to work hard, play to your strengths, and make the most of the strengths of those around you.

The worksheet that follows can help you summarize everything you've learned about yourself in this part of the book. Remember that career development and management is an ongoing process and does not end here. Use what you've learned about yourself to guide you as your career journey unfolds.

# Part IV Summary: Take Action

In this section, you identified strengths and weaknesses of your job search style and identified specific strategies for improving your job search. You have also looked at your emotional intelligence and considered ways to be a more effective team member and worker.

Based on the results of the assessments and the information you completed in each chapter, use the following worksheet to summarize what you've discovered about yourself. You can then use this information to further assess your career plan and, more importantly, to put that plan into action. By pulling together your results from all three chapters, you should have a much better sense of what steps you need to take to achieve career success and satisfaction.

## EXERCISE

Job search strategies I can improve on (from chapter 10):

_____

_____

What I can do now to make my job search more effective:

_____

_____

My preferred job search style (from chapter 11): _____

Strengths of my job search style:

_____

_____

Weaknesses of my job search style and ways to improve them:

_____

_____

Emotional intelligence skills I can improve on (from chapter 12):

_____

_____

Ways I can be more effective and successful at work:

_____

_____

_____

_____

# Conclusion

Congratulations!

You have done a lot of hard work, learned a lot about yourself and your connection with the world of work, and, hopefully, have found your ideal job so you can start down your newly envisioned career path. Remember, you need to carefully manage your career because it will not manage itself. You may want to take the assessments in this book again in about six months to see if your needs, interests, skills, or values have changed; to make sure that you're still in balance; to see if entrepreneurship looks more appealing; or to simply find more ways to be successful at work. If so, you may also need to make new career decisions, set new career goals, and find different ways to implement changes. Whether you crack open this book again or not, never forget the advice of Socrates that started this book, and learn as much about yourself as possible.

Oliver Wendell Holmes once said, "Greatness is not in where we stand, but in what direction we are moving. We must sail sometimes with the wind and sometimes against it—but sail we must and not drift, nor lie at anchor."

Keep sailing.

# Index

# C

# Notes

# Notes

# Notes